GOD'S PARTY

A Guide to New Forms of Worship

GOD'S PARTY

A Guide to New Forms of Worship

David James Randolph

Nashville   ABINGDON PRESS   New York

GOD'S PARTY: A GUIDE TO NEW FORMS OF WORSHIP

Copyright © 1975 by Abingdon Press

Library of Congress Cataloging in Publication Data

RANDOLPH, DAVID JAMES, 1934-   God's party. Bibliography: p. 1. Public worship. I. Title.
BV15.R36   264   74-18293

ISBN 0-687-15445-6

Material on pp. 129-33 is reprinted from Sanctuary Planning,
prepared by the staff of the Department of Architecture, Norman
G. Byar, Executive Secretary, Copyright 1967 by the National
Division of the Board of Missions of the Methodist Church. Used
by permission of the Office of Architecture, National Division,
Board of Global Ministries of the United Methodist Church.

Material from *Ventures in Worship I*, edited by David J. Randolph,
copyright © 1969 by Abingdon Press, is used by permission.

The illustration of page 12 is reprinted from *Rock and Other Four
Letter Words: Music of the Electric Generation,* written and designed by J Marks, photographed by Linda Eastman; copyright ©
1968 by J Marks. Published by Bantam Books, Inc.

Scripture quotations noted RSV are from the Revised Standard
Version of the Bible, copyrighted 1946, 1952, and 1971, by the
Division of Christian Education, National Council of Churches,
and are used by permission.

MANUFACTURED BY THE PARTHENON PRESS AT
NASHVILLE, TENNESSEE, UNITED STATES OF AMERICA

To
David III and Tracey
Who constantly guide Juanita and me
To new forms of living

Acknowledgments

There are many people to whom I should like to express thanks. That in itself would virtually fill a volume. Certainly to the members of the Committee on the Project on Worship from 1968 to 1972, I want to express my thanks. I also want to express appreciation to the many persons who have shared their insights with me in seminars and workshops all over the country. Especially, I remember the groups that met at the Convocation on Worship in St. Louis and Workshops on Worship in Texas, New Hampshire, Mississippi, California, Ohio, New York, Oregon, and elsewhere. I am also very grateful for the opportunity to have worked in the field of worship in the National Council of Churches, and I hope the ecumenical intention of this work will be as evident in these pages as it is in the Project itself. Thanks are due Hoyt Hickman, who offered helpful comments. Bishop William Cannon and Bishop Mack Stokes read chapter 3 and offered encouragement. Dr. Harold DeWolf also read this chapter and made suggestions. Of course I am responsible for the material presented here. To Mrs. Ursa Worthy, who started typing these pages, I am especially grateful, as I am to her spirited successor, Mrs. Everland Robinson.

Contents

*Worship celebrates the vitality by which
we enjoy life*
*Worship celebrates the values by which we
govern life*
*Worship celebrates the visions by which
we transform life*

New Shapes of Celebration

Time and place
Acts of worship

Analysis
The Lord's Supper: models of change
There are changes in language
There are changes in structure
*There are changes in the style of the ser-
vice*

Factors in the Transformation of Worship

A renewed sense of the reality of God
*The emergence of a revolutionary under-
standing of liturgy*

Contents

Experimental
Simple, Balanced by the Values of Complexity
Clear, Balanced by the Values of Ambiguity
Concrete

Weddings
Baptisms
Funerals

The Creative Process
Steps to More Meaningful Worship

Worship
Study in small groups
*Gather data from the congregation and
  others*
Review and create resources
Design the service
Worship again
Evaluate
Worship!

Behold, the former things have
    come to pass,
  and new things I now declare;
before they spring forth
  I tell you of them.

              Isaiah 42:9 RSV

        We are all . . .
        participants
        in the eternal
        joy play
        multi leveled
        energy being
        celebration

        Bernard Gunther

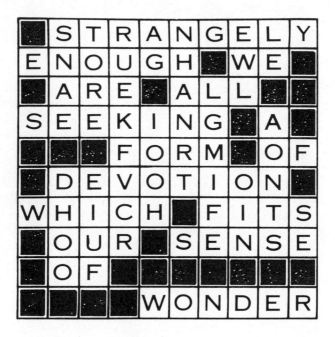

Introduction

We are in the midst of a worship explosion that is likely to become even more dynamic in the years ahead. Explosion is not too strong a word, for what is happening in liturgy today is bursting forth in new forms of life while at the same time leaving unwanted repercussions in some quarters.

What is the *point* of this liturgical explosion? What is its mood? What forces are behind it? What are we learning in it? After a time of guitars and leotards, when anything new seemed good, what genuine values are emerging in the current liturgical explorations? What are the criteria by which we may distinguish between the new forms of worship? Why is it that new forms of worship have been a path to renewed congregational life in some places and merely controversial activities in others? And how may a local church go about finding its own new way of worship? These are some of the questions with which we seek to deal in this volume.

It is with the sense that we are at the beginning of an era that these pages are prepared. I believe that the current movement in the worship life of the church will be as significant historically as such epochal events as the Protestant Reformation. I say this because to me the most significant thing about our contemporary worship lies not in mod liturgies, jazz masses, and new music and dances in themselves, but in the way in which liturgy is becoming the work of the people in the preparation of the worship. In the unprecedented fashion in which the people are helping to develop the resources with which they praise God lies the key to the dramatic revolution in worship in our time. This revolution is the work not so much of a few "stars" but of a great band of people, ministers and laymen, all across the church, in small congregations as well as large, who are opening themselves to the Spirit of God and finding new ways of praise and service.

The point of what is happening will be missed if people see only changes in language or movement of furniture. Forms are not an end in themselves. The ultimate task of the renewal of worship will lie not in the development of new forms but in the creation of new people.

The purpose of this work is to analyze contemporary worship and to suggest guidelines for the future.

The focus of this work is on the parish church, the local congregation. Its intention is to be helpful to persons at the local level, both clergy and lay, who seek more meaningful worship. I have tried to deal with the salient features and major issues of contemporary worship as they have been raised by different people, but I have tried to draw the many comments into one larger conversation.

In chapter 1, we consider the main theme of contemporary worship; seek to characterize it, sketch its shape, and consider the forces that are shaping it, along with some of its limitations.

In chapter 2, we inquire into the goals of worship, and in chapter 3, the criteria by which we discern meaningful Christian worship.

Chapter 4 attempts to confront the basic theological issue for worship—the relationship of the reality of God and the realities of daily life—and to explore the possibility of a new liturgical language by which these realities may come together.

Chapter 5 inquires further into verbal language and its relation to human being and acting.

Chapter 6 sketches attempts to make weddings, baptisms, and funerals more meaningful.

Chapter 7 summarizes what we are learning about the process of change in worship at the local level.

Chapter 8 offers a pattern by which a local church may assess its worship, become aware of resources, and exercise options toward more meaningful worship.

Each chapter may not be of equal interest or relevance to each congregation, but I hope the careful reader will see the relatedness of the concerns under discussion.

One of the most remarkable aspects of contemporary worship is the way in which the practice of many churches and the theory of many scholars converge at significant points. I hope these points of convergence will become evident as the study proceeds and the interrelatedness of the chapters will become clear, even though the reader's primary focus may be in one of the other areas. It is hoped that the empirical data will be of as much interest to scholars as the theoretical considerations are to laymen.

This study attempts to consider new liturgical forms as expressions of living theology and explores ways in which theological guidelines may be applied to worship. I hope it may help continue the necessary task of relating worship and theology in a vital and life-transforming way.

The word "new" as it is being used here refers essentially to materials of current or recent origin that are unfamiliar to the public. "New" is, of course, a relative term. What is new to one congregation may be old to another. There are some examples of literally ancient material that have been included in the *Ventures* series because their significance has been newly discovered or because, although the materials are old, they are not familiar to many people.

There are many limitations to this study in addition to the ones that the author brings. This work is limited primarily to local parish churches, although some materials are drawn from campus ministries and other specialized ministries. The influence of the worship of the black community is very strong on these pages, although it is indirect. This study will not deal directly with worship in the black community, and worship among racial and ethnic minorities because this material is currently under study and we expect future publications that will specialize in these areas.

Obviously such a work is a "report from the field," and makes no pretense of being exhaustive. Contemporary worship is so much in ferment that attempts to codify it would be inappropriate even if they were possible. This report is rather an exploration of fundamental issues based upon more than five years of gathering data from parish churches all over the United States and from a few other countries, plus a continuing dialogue with scholars in the field of liturgics.

The Project on Worship is the instrumentality through which this research was initiated. The goals of the Project, which the author directs at 1908 Grand Avenue, Nashville, Tennessee 37203, are to collect, evaluate, share, stimulate and create resources for contemporary worship. The *Ventures in Worship* series published by Abingdon Press is an expression of the Project. The work continues. Contributions of acts of worship, case studies, theological reflection, and insight are welcome.

1 God's Party

The worship of the Christian church should be like a party for which God is host and to which everyone is invited. Worship is the celebration of the good news that man has a sponsor in the universe and a fellowship on earth. Jesus Christ said as much in the parable of the great feast (Luke 14:15-24; cf. Matt. 22:1-10), and the church at its best has understood Christ himself to be the life of the party.

Jesus likened life in the kingdom to a great feast. The image appeals to most of us because one of the most pleasant experiences of life is to attend a party thrown by a gracious host where we are among friends. We greet one another warmly, enjoy good food, talk over old times, share the good news and the bad, take a look at the future, and open ourselves to new possibilities. A distinctive element in this party in the parable is that an active invitation is extended to the outsider. The waiter is sent out to bring in people off the streets. Therein lies the embarrassment, and to this we must return. But the major point is clear: Jesus intends our fellowship with God and with one another to be a great celebration. This is the joyous revelation that lies at the heart of the current revolution in worship.

To celebrate is simply to make public our faith.

Thus for centuries the Mass has been celebrated. But to celebrate is also to rejoice in the faith, even in the midst of suffering and death. Indeed, what else does "celebrating the Mass" mean? When we consider the cause for celebration we begin to get a grasp of why people today are understanding worship as God's party.

Worship celebrates the vitality by which we enjoy life. God is the Creator, Redeemer, and Sustainer of life. Jesus himself must have been one of the most vital persons who ever lived. The records of him show that he experienced life to the full. He found enjoyment in the everyday things of life. He was a fabulous storyteller who could keep people spellbound for hours. He enjoyed food and good company. He must have loved to laugh—when he cried it was so unusual they wrote it down, "Jesus wept." And he did weep. He mourned. He suffered. He died. But even the worst that men could do could not keep him down. People found his presence with them, and they said it all in a few words: "In him was life. . . ."

Worship in the presence of such a Lord partakes of his vitality. Inspired by this, contemporary worship moves out of locked-in forms to more open styles of celebration.

People are more likely to be encouraged to drink coffee and talk to one another before a service than to "enter in silence." The leader is more likely to be robed in a "hallelujah poncho" or other bright colors than in a black robe. The music is likely to invite a dance rather than a dirge. Instead of blocking themselves off in rigid rows, persons may reach out to touch one another, even embrace. A visitor to such a service might say of the worshipers, "In them was life."

Worship celebrates the values by which we govern life. In Luke's Gospel, Jesus follows the parable of the feast by discussing the cost of discipleship. When one becomes a disciple of Jesus Christ he says "yes" to Christ the Lord and "no" to anything that stands in the way. At

the center of the Christian party there is no cake. There is
a cross.

The cross first, then discipleship. Christ the Lord,
then family. These are hard words. But they express
reality. We live by values, and values demand choice.
Choice demands selectivity. Christian worship holds up
the values by which we live, in the light of which we
make our choices. Thus there is a hard moral core at the
center of genuine worship. We are brought up hard
against our sins and wickedness. Love stands over
against our hate. Truth stands over against our lies. Justice stands over against our personal, ecclesiastical, social, and national immoralities. The values of the Christian faith are often hard to live with. But it is harder still
to try to live without them. This is what the Christian
finds when he counts the cost of coming to God's party.

Worship celebrates the visions by which we transform life. In Luke's gospel, Jesus' discussion of the feast
and discipleship leads to the parable of the tower. We
have a vision. We see a tower rising up above the mists
of the present. We pay the price. We build the tower.

We live by our visions, and Christian worship seeks
to supply them in such a way that life may be transformed. "Where there is no vision, the people perish"
(Proverbs 29:18).

A person cannot live without a vision. Tell me your
address, your phone number, and I will know a little
about you. But tell me your dreams, what you hope for,
and I will know more. Where do you see yourself a year
from now? Five years? Tell me that, and I will know
something about you. But *who* will you be a year from
now? Five years? Tell me how you see yourself changing
and who you see yourself becoming, and I will know
much about you.

A local church cannot live without a vision. No
matter how comforting the past and present may be,
unless there is a growing edge of nurture and outreach
the congregation shrivels inwardly and outwardly.

A nation cannot live without a vision. The United States of America became great when it had a great vision. Men, women, and children came from across the world because they had a new vision of what life could be in this good land. Inspired by a vision of the good life, they pushed back the frontiers and broke the plains. At this point in history, as we enter the bicentennial era of the United States, we are painfully aware that we have been disobedient to our best visions and that even our visions may have been flawed. We must discover and create a new vision of who we are and what we are to do in the world, or we shall perish.

Worship deals in visions. Worship holds up before us an image of who we most truly are and what we may become—as persons, as a church, as a nation. And worship transmits the power by which life can be transformed: new persons in a new church for a new world.

New Shapes of Celebration

Imagine a modern-day Rip Van Winkle who has been asleep for twenty years and wanders into church on Sunday morning. What will he find? There is no way to answer this question unequivocally, and this is a main point of what is now happening in worship: services now vary significantly from place to place as congregations find their own liturgical style. Of course there are exceptions. Our Rip may step into some churches and find little or nothing changed. However, so widespread is the contemporary worship exploration that he would more than likely find dramatic changes. New shapes of celebration can be found in every aspect of worship and in its totality.

Time and place. First, the visitor might appear in a church on a Thursday evening to find a service of worship as people get ready to leave their hometowns for the weekend. Or he might find worship at 9:00 A.M. rather than at 11:00 A.M. on Sunday—and in a fellowship hall rather than in a sanctuary. Chairs might be arranged in circles rather than in rows, and for large parts of the service they might be pushed back to the edges while people sat on the floor and talked, drew pictures, or did finger paintings. He might walk into a church where there were several different services of worship in different styles going on simultaneously. Or he might show up at a neighbor's house on a weeknight and find Holy Communion being celebrated—at the kitchen table.

Acts of worship. As the service began, the voice that called to worship might be that of a woman or a layman. If it were an ordained clergyman it would not be in a formal "stained-glass tone." Instead of Gothic words he might hear:

Leader: In a time of sorrow, a time of despair;

People: We have come to celebrate the Word.

Leader: In a time of confusion with our world in turmoil and our lives torn between issues;

People: We gather as a congregation to celebrate the Word.

Leader: In a time when our various worlds are hungering and thirsting for love, forgiveness, grace, and goodness;

People: We have come to rededicate our lives to the task of putting our flesh in the Word.[1]

or

Leader: We have this special opportunity today to join as a community in celebration and thanksgiving of the lives we have been given.

People: We thank God for this gift and wish to become faithful servants and givers of His grace and love.

Leader: Let us use this hour of divine Worship to call

our lives into question and to go from this place new persons.

People: We thank God for His renewing spirit that works wonders in our lives through people who give of themselves daily.[2]

The declaration of faith may have come out of the congregation's own quest and be read responsively, like this:

Leader: In the midst of flashing neon darkness,

People: We dare this day to celebrate the light.

Leader: In the midst of blaring, shouting silence,

People: We dare this day to celebrate the word.

Leader: In the midst of bloated, gorged starvation,

People: We dare this day to celebrate the bread.

Leader: In the midst of bottled, bubbling thirst,

People: We dare this day to celebrate the water.

Leader: In the midst of smothered, gnawing doubt,

People: We dare to celebrate the affirmation.

Leader: In the midst of frantic, laughing death,

People: We dare this day to celebrate the life.

Leader: Sing alleluia—rejoice!
       . . . with trembling.[3]

When time came for prayer, instead of bowing his head he might be invited to hold the hands of those near him and look into their eyes while the leader prayed.

The scripture might be read responsively, perhaps in dialogue with a copy from the morning's newspaper.

The music might be from the top-forty charts, perhaps played on stereo. A group of young musicians with electrified instruments might do the anthem. Electronic music might be played in a highly sophisticated congregation.

The proclamation could be delivered by one person about midway through the service, or it might be a brief address early in the service. It might not be a monologue at all. The sermon could be in such forms as these:

Poetry
Parable, or short story
A film
A 35mm slide presentation
A combination of media
A fantasy exercise
A dance, or "rhythmic movement"
A videotape

Our visitor might be awakened by such language to new insights. Or he might wonder if and how these acts fit together. Looking at his bulletin (perhaps illustrated by a local artist) instead of an "Order of Worship" he might find that the service was arranged in a more dynamic, missional pattern such as the following:

An Order for Morning Worship

The Church Gathers

Prelude
Call to Worship (Introit)
    Sing to the Lord a new song
    Sing his praise from the end of the earth
    Sing to the Lord, bless his name
    Tell of his salvation from day to day
    Declare his glory among the nations
    His marvelous works among all the peoples.
Hymn
Invocation
Call to Confession
Prayer of Confession
    Father, you are the source of all joy and happiness. Yet we your children have looked elsewhere and satisfied ourselves with cheap im-

itation pleasures. We have sought thrills and
outward ease, missing the peace and inward
contentment that you offer. We have let the
world squeeze us into its mold. We have let
Madison Avenue dictate our tastes and Hol-
lywood our desires. Forgive us, O God, and
remold us in your image, so that we may rejoice in knowing you through your Son Jesus
Christ.

Personal Confessions—Amen
  Words of Assurance
  The Lord's Prayer—modern version

To Hear the Word of God

Call to Praise
Psalter 569: Psalm 42
Gloria Patri
Anthem: "The Big, Bright, Green Pleasure
    Machine"
Old Testament Lesson
New Testament Lesson
Hymn 67, "The King of Love My Shepherd Is"
    Psalm 23
Sermon: On "Richard Cory" (Simon & Garfunk-
    el)
Silent Reflection

To Respond in Faith

Affirmation of Faith
Call to Prayer
Prayer of Thanksgiving
Prayer of Petition
Personal Prayers
Collect
  Merciful God, who has taught us to seek first
  your kingdom, unbend our wills, that we may
  find everything good in serving you and our

fellowmen. Through Jesus Christ our Lord.
Amen.
Parish Notices
Offering
Doxology
Prayer of Dedication

The Church Scatters

Call to Service
Hymn
Benediction
Postlude, "What Must I Do? How Must I Live?"[4]

Analysis

We hope our visitor would remain for continuing
fellowship with the congregation. He might talk to the
pastor and to members of the committee that had helped
prepare the service. They could discuss the service and
what might come from it.

If we look beneath the surface of the events represented above, all of which took place in actual worshiping congregations, we can see three fundamental
types of changes that have taken place in the shift from
traditional worship.

The pattern of worship may remain relatively un-
changed, but traditional language is exchanged for contemporary. This is the mildest and perhaps the most
widespread form of liturgical change. However, this
does not come easy if the task is seen as interpreting
abiding meanings in contemporary terms and not just
substituting new words for old.

The basic order of the elements of worship may be
changed as well as their language.

Here I refer to the whole way in which worship is
conceived and carried out. There is a new consciousness
of what worship is, of what its sources are, and a new

variety of environments and actions that expresses worship.

The Lord's Supper: models of change. Let us focus now on the Lord's Supper, the central act of Christian worship, to see how these types of change express themselves in some current thinking and acting out of worship.

Although the sacramental meal is called by several names in different traditions, the basic content of the service is largely the same:

1. Remembrance
2. Proclamation
3. Offertory
4. Participation
5. Thanksgiving[5]

With all the weight of tradition and apparent consensus, however, the Lord's Supper has nonetheless seemed drained of meaning to many persons who deliberately stay away from church when they know that this sacrament is being celebrated. Changes in language, structure, and style are being attempted in a quest for meaning.

There are changes in language. One form of change has been to maintain the structure of a traditional liturgy but to update the choice of words.

For example, James Righter, a United Methodist pastor in Virginia, was troubled because he found the traditional Communion service so lacking in meaning for many of the members of the church he was serving. He deliberately set out in pastoral calling to discover just what the problems were in the traditional service and how they might be corrected. Again and again he discovered that the words of the traditional service were blocks to communication. He therefore sought to develop what he called "A Communion Service in Modern English."[6] To get the flavor of the service that came out of this dialogue with the congregation, consider this

Invitation to Communion, General Prayer of Confession, and Words of Assurance:

Invitation to Communion . . . . .The Minister
Friends, if you sincerely turn your back on your sins; if you want to live in love and peace with everyone; if you desire to lead a new life doing God's will from now on; then prepare to come forward in faith to receive this sacrament. Now let us make our peace with God, confident of his forgiveness, by joining in this prayer of confession:

General Prayer of Confession (all seated and bowed in prayer):
O God, whom Jesus called Father, we admit that we have done many wrong and wicked things. We admit that we have ignored many opportunities to do the loving thing. We are sorry that we have thought, said, and done such foolishness. Now we turn away from our mistakes. We are sick at heart, Father, when we think of them. Forgive us for not knowing what we do. Please forgive us. In the name of Jesus, forgive us. Grant that we may so love and serve you all our days, that others will praise you. Amen.

Words of Assurance .The Minister
God our Father has promised to forgive all who turn to him in faith. Even now he forgives us, and sets us free to live new lives in Jesus Christ our Lord. Henceforth we may live, not in fear or dread, but secure in his power and love. Nothing can separate us from the love of Christ. Therefore, let us rejoice in the Lord our God!

There are changes in structure. The type of approach followed by Righter has found wide acceptance among laymen, although Righter himself has revised the service in his continuing dialogue with laymen and with scholars. Variations of this approach are fairly common with adaptations of language being made in terms of the particular community in which the liturgy takes place.

However, some have been critical of this approach because they feel it simply makes linguistic alterations without dealing with the more fundamental issue of the structure of the service itself. Some believe that the traditional United Methodist Order of Holy Communion is deficient at the point of genuine celebration of thanksgiving. In an Alternate Ritual the "thanksgiving" was added following the Offering and prior to the Sanctus.

The Thanksgiving:

Call to Thanksgiving	The Lord be with you. *And also with you.* Lift up your hearts. *We lift them up to the Lord.* Let us give thanks to the Lord our God. *It is right to give him thanks and praise.*
Preface	Father, it is fitting that we should always and everywhere give you thanks and praise. Only you are God. You are the source of all that is good. You created earth and space, all that lives, and us who bear your image. Even when we rebelled against your love, you did not desert us. You delivered us from captivity, made covenant to be our God and King, and taught us through prophets. Therefore, in union with the company of heaven and all your people now on earth, we worship and glorify you as we sing (say):

Holy, holy,	*Holy, holy, holy, Lord, God of power and might,*
	heaven and earth are full of your glory.
	  Hosanna in the highest.
	Blessed is he who comes in the name of the Lord.
	  Hosanna in the highest.[7]

There are changes in the style of the service. The structural change just mentioned enriches the service of Holy Communion by making more explicit the element of thanksgiving, which surely was present in the original act. There may be further such structural redevelopments, as there are sure to be continued experiments with the word choice in services such as Righter developed. However, changes in word choice and structure do not necessarily get at the root of the difficulty for the Lord's Supper or for worship more broadly. The problem as I have tried to outline it here is that the reality of the services of worship and the reality of daily life fail to coincide for many people.

The problem is not how to *write* "Thanks" into the service but how thanksgiving is to be genuinely understood, felt, expressed in the service of worship and appropriated into the ongoing processes of life. At this point rubrics become especially important. The arrangement of the congregation, the architecture itself, the lighting, the timing of the service, the pace, the means of personal interaction—all these factors affect what happens or does not happen in the service of worship.

The Sacrament of the Lord's Supper should help us discern that God's activity in the world around us offers more in worship than merely concerns that are to be prayed over. Are there not also elements of praise here? And thanksgiving? Why, when the offering is present, should the congregation bring only bread and money? Why should not children bring posters they have drawn, women something they have knitted, or men something they have made, or a student an essay he has written? Why could not a committee report from a group in the church be brought forward? There can be more links between the realities of worship and the realities of our common life.

All these matters are matters of *style*—ways in which the reality of the event comes to expression. And

this is the area in which every congregation finds its
own way of living liturgically.

One example of the way in which a particular congregation expressed the reality of its life in its own
liturgical style at Communion comes from Faith Baptist
Church in Georgetown, Kentucky.[8] The pastor, Roger
Lovette, writes about this particular service:

I want you, now . . . to look at the web of your relationships right now. And I want you to ask . . . just how our chair
arrangement fits you . . . and fits our church. Should you sit
like this all the time with your mate—because it best expresses
who you are? Is this the way you relate to your children . . . to
your neighbors . . .? I never will forget a play I saw in New
York years ago. It was called *Separate Tables*. It told the story
of people who sat down to a great banquet feast—at separate
tables. It was a story of loneliness—and estrangement.

That is not the Table of the Lord. At this Table—we are
brothers and sisters—seeking to know and to be known
—whatever the difficulties and the hardships. We can never sit
down to the Great Banquet Feast he holds out at separate tables
. . . it is just not possible. Either we break the bread
together—or not at all.

And so right now . . . I want you to take that piece of paper
attached to your program . . . and make your confession. Confess whatever estrangement that you know . . . and you feel . . .
whatever you have done to deepen the chasms that divide us
here . . . and how you have ignored that mandate he gave us.
And when you have made that confession . . . would you come
forward, drop it in the offering plate . . . and then return to your
seat. As you return . . . quietly turn your chair around . . . for
you are now ready to come to the Table. The last parable he
ever told . . . he told about a man who asked the question:
"Lord, when did we see you?" Do you recall his answer? "I
was a stranger and you welcomed me."

This particular means of celebrating the Lord's
Supper might not be as effective if done regularly, and it
might not be appropriate in every congregation. But it
does dramatize that search for authenticity and the style
of expression through which every congregation must
go if the worship of the church is to be a time when we
are "no longer strangers."

God's Party

Factors in the Transformation of Worship

Why are changes such as these taking place with increasing rapidity? Consider some of the factors that are helping to transform worship in our time, not necessarily in the order of their importance.

1. *A renewed sense of the reality of God.* The "God is dead" theology of a few years past may have had its moment of truth, but it was short-lived. For a time people seemed stunned by that claim, then it was almost as if a quiet whisper rose to a great shout, "God is alive!" The awareness of the reality of God seemed heightened by the attempt to claim his demise. The reaction was as untutored as the rehearsal of old songs, "He lives, He lives, He lives within my heart!" It was as sophisticated as Peter Berger's study of the transcendent, *A Rumor of Angels.* [9] But it was deep, and it continues to grow. At the base of the transformation of worship in our time is a vital sense of the reality of the God who is being worshiped. There is cause for celebration!

2. *The emergence of a revolutionary understanding of liturgy.* The literary critic Kenneth Burke once observed that in the period following the American Civil War the language of the churches was a rhetoric of consolation. After the tragedy of the War Between the States the primary purpose of the church seemed to be that of healing, of binding up the wounds. There is a good deal of evidence to support Burke's thesis right into our own time. Then with the rise of black consciousness and the Vietnamese war a dramatic change took place. Suddenly the church became a place not only for the rhetoric of *consolation* but the rhetoric of *confrontation.* Suddenly there was James Forman confronting the congregation with the demands of the black manifesto. Suddenly there were nuns stretched out on the floor of the cathedral protesting the war in Vietnam. And suddenly a dimension of biblical faith that had eluded Americans for almost a century was back at the center of our cultic

life: worship is a time for confrontation as well as consolation. The God who is with us and for us is also over
against us in his demand for justice and for peace. If that
awareness belonged only to a few people like those who
demonstrated so forcefully it would have passed with
the time. None of those demonstrations was especially
fruitful as a means of achieving the end desired; but at
that time, and no doubt under the stimulus of certain
dramatic acts, the basic truth of worship as confrontation
was dawning upon many people. Thus in their prayers
of confession, as well as in hymns and sermons, the
dimension of social responsibility was working its way
into the center of worship. This has created tension, as it
should. There should be a tension between consolation
and confrontation in worship, for both of these are
legitimate and necessary aspects of the worship of the
God of biblical faith. We can find ways of helping the
tension be creative, but we are likely to be living with it
for a long time. It took us at least a century to get into this
situation, and it may take us a century to work our way
through. We hope not. There are signs of healing in the
midst of confrontation.

3. *The impact of biblical studies.* Biblical studies by
professional scholars and lay persons have flourished
since World War II. Not all the hopes for biblical studies
have been realized, and as yet no single "biblical theology" has developed as a rallying point for the Christian
cause. However, what the biblical studies have done is to
show a sense of the enormous vitality and range of expression by means of which men and women may seek
God and praise him. The dynamic of the biblical understanding of life has exploded the little boxes of
rationalistic thought and polite middle-class convention
in which many people kept their ideas about God and
man. That explosion has shaken the house of worship
and cleared the way for a fresh approach to our expressions of prayer and praise.

4. *The development of phenomenological thought.*

That way of thinking known as phenomenology, flowing from Edmund Husserl and others, has made a remarkable impact upon our understanding of worship. More will be said about this later (see chapter 4 on "The Real Issue"). However, I mention phenomenology as a major factor at this point because it has helped clarify the philosophical framework for worship in an era when the traditional understandings drawn from Greek metaphysics and classical philosophical thought have been steadily eroded by a new consciousness of human life. There are still many persons who are not yet consciously aware of the need, which is being forced both by contemporary science and current events to return to the foundations of thought. Among those who do have this perception, however, phenomenology has emerged as a way of thinking through issues that seem to have been blocked by other philosophical approaches. For example, the subject-object dichotomy raises the question of subjectivity and objectivity in worship. Phenomenological method offers a valid and exciting alternative for the future.

5. *The fresh growth of the body of literature on worship.* Phenomenological thought has not been the only style that has had a "greening" effect on worship. A number of books from different perspectives has rather suddenly turned what had been a fairly esoteric subject into one of considerable public interest. Just to mention some authors and titles (fuller information is given in the Bibliography, pages 135-38) is to get a sense of the range of excitement of recent literature in this field: Harvey Cox, *The Feast of Fools*; Sam Keen, *Apology for Wonder*; Robert Neale, *In Praise of Play*; Paul Hoon, *The Integrity of Worship*; and there are others.

6. *New developments in communication.* We are entering a new age, and it is an age of communications. No one is quite sure just what such a claim means, although it is made with increasing frequency. We sense something of what is coming when we realize that a

major part of the great achievement of man's moon journeys has been not just that he went to the moon but that he was able to tell the story and share the pictures as he journeyed. That picture of the earth as seen from outer space gives reality to the phrase "spaceship earth" and is an expression of this new age of communications. It says more to us than words alone could ever do. This new age of communication permeates us and affects us even while we are not aware of it. Those of us who came on stage while such media as the film or television were rising to prominence feel this but perhaps not as deeply as the children who have grown up in the multi-media age. Our new range of media is open to them, and they tend to use them quite unselfconsciously, making an audio tape, taking a picture, experimenting with a video machine, photocopying. These and many other expressions are becoming as common as the 35mm. slide shown in the home. Increasingly we are coming to take these multi-media expressions for granted in worship as well. It is becoming more and more common to see projected art or hear recorded music in church. This is only the beginning of an era that will see an almost infinite expansion of the possibilities of communication in worship.

7. *Fresh approaches to education.* The way contemporary education is expressing our changing consciousness is evident in the gap between many "traditional" services of worship and young people who are either not in church any longer or desperately tormented by it. However this situation is not as common as it once was because the new approaches to education have increasingly made their way into worship itself, tending to bring revitalization with them. A participatory style of education in which students are partners with the teacher leads to a participatory style of worship in which laymen and clergy are partners in worship. The growing awareness of who the learner is has taught us ways of sensitizing ourselves in worship. In learning how fan-

tasy may help us understand ourselves or relate to our world, fantasizing has been recovered as an element in worship. Many of these developments are not necessarily "new" but they have been new in a context of education that has tended to be rationalistic and worship that has followed in that pattern. Generations educated in these new ways will want to worship in new ways with a fresh sense of wonder and discovery.

8. *The vitality of the contemporary arts.* The first thing to be observed here is simply the current liveliness of the lively arts. In spite of continuing public failure to support the arts adequately the artists are hurling their creative works before us and often leading us to new insights and visions. Moreover, there seems to be an openness to religion on the part of artists who only a few years ago were thoroughly disenchanted. Now the Christian story is gripping the creative imagination once again. We see this in such varied forms as Leonard Bernstein's *Mass,* the stage and film versions of *Jesus Christ Superstar* and *Godspell,* the dance of the Apostles' Creed, as performed by Lyn Seymour of the Royal Ballet, the willingness of artists to participate in consultations dealing with faith, and in many other ways. There is a special flowering in the field of liturgical arts, those arts which create expressly for ritual acts, as seen in banners, vestments, crosses, etc., as well as music and dance. Religious architecture at its best continues to be in the forefront of its field, and the religious crafts are highly active and visible. The vitality of the contemporary arts helps enrich and transform worship at many different levels.

9. *The emergence of ethnic awareness.* Worship as it had been practiced in main-line Protestant denominations in America, up through the 1950's anyway, had been relatively one-dimensional. It is not quite fair to call it Anglo-Saxon because even that ethnic force seemed bleached out of much worship. Then came the concern for the black: black awareness, black conscious-

ness, black power. As the black recovered his African heritage it stimulated others to turn to their own roots and recover that power which had been evaporated in a cultural pressure cooker. When attention was turned to the black church it was turned to worship. Many people who had discarded the role of worship and personal piety in favor of social action were astonished by the primary and pervasive role of worship in the black community. That "soul" which permeates black worship has reached out and touched most other worship as well. It has helped Hispanic people to affirm their uniqueness, as for example in the Mariachi Mass, and it is helping Anglo-Saxons as well to realize that their heritage is much broader and more colorful than the nineteenth-century version of it seemed to be. We probably will continue to see an emphasis on the ethnic, hopefully as a prelude to a new ecumenical understanding of worship.

10. *The contributions of creative individuals and communities.* The term "transformation of worship" is inconceivable without the outpouring of the talents of many individuals and communities. Not all of them are identifiable ethnically. It is not easy to trace their influence, to know just how it developed or how great it is, but certainly some people in extending the boundaries of worship—even if at times they seemed to others to go too far—have greatly enriched our situation. We think of such persons as Pope John XXIII and such communities as the Roman Catholic Church. The Constitution on the Sacred Liturgy coming out of the second Vatican Council has had an enormous influence on the vitalization of worship everywhere. And what Pope John did in his colossal way others have done in the ways open to them. The list is expandable, and as each of us makes up our own we sense our indebtedness to those who have patrolled the boundaries and widened them for us.

11. *The focus on the church in its local expression.* After an era in which the church was not taken very

seriously and almost discarded by some in favor of "secular strategies," the growing interest in the church has helped move worship into the center of discussion. As we look at the church in its local expression we see that a basic intuition of the masses of faithful laymen is valid. Worship does lie at the center of life. In the process of renewing their worship many congregations have found new life, and in the process of finding new life many congregations have found new worship. One of the most striking aspects of the contemporary transformation of worship is that *it has arisen at the local level.* That new worship which is the subject of this volume had its origin primarily in the life of congregations in the day-to-day, week-to-week worship of God and exploration of his mission. The contemporary surge of interest in worship has its origin not in the libraries of the scholars nor the visions of futurologists, although both have contributed. Rather, in the confrontation of the church with the world in its particular concrete manifestation, a new way of discovering the reality of God and expressing the meaning of the encounter has been worked out in what we call new ways of worship. All the above theological and cultural developments might have moved on by the church were it not for the awareness and creativity of numbers of pastors and laymen who were able to catch fresh meanings of God in our day and to celebrate them in worship.

So, Sunday will never be the same, nor will our lives and our world, if the promise of a new worship comes true.

Embarrassments

Changes are not necessarily for the better. Even the most ardent advocates of new ways are aware of embarrassments that keep worship from being truly God's party.

One embarrassment is precisely the one Jesus

warned about in the parable of the great feast—*those who are invited often seem unwilling or unable to communicate the reality of faith* in such a way that the outsiders are drawn to the Christian fellowship. Worship, after all, does not take place for the self-gratification of the few but for the service of the world. To be sure, there is evidence that new ways of worship do serve as evangelism and lead to social action. The embarrassment is that there is not more evidence that demonstrates how changed worship changes people and communities.

Another embarrassment is that changes in worship can be disruptive when they are undertaken without some process of planned change. If the outburst of creativity is a major plus sign of contemporary worship, our lack of understanding of the most fruitful ways to initiate and develop change is a major minus sign.

Failure to deal with basic theological issues is a weakness in some cases. We note "in some cases" because generally the leaders of creative worship have been theologically literate and perceptive as well as innovative. The picture some critics have drawn of untutored novices mindlessly creating new forms I believe to be an inaccurate and unfortunate cartoon. As I try to show elsewhere in this volume, there is a seriously constructive theological effort behind most innovative worship. Granting this, however, much of this theological effort has been implicit and needs to be made more explicit. Criticism of that effort should help to refine it. Surely abstract criticism will not halt it.

Not all the efforts at creative worship are of equal value. As in every human venture the quality of work varies. In this moment of history we do need to encourage creativity. Acts of worship from a given setting may work in that setting (or they may not). However, there are criteria of excellence in expression and execution that need to be met if material of highest value is to be produced.

There are serious gaps in our explorations. For example, there are still few "case studies" of change in particular congregations, or of specific services.[10] And the whole relationship of cult and culture is in need of fresh exploration.

There are other embarrassments that can no doubt be added to this list. But even when such a list is extended and taken seriously, I am more attracted by the invitation to God's party than I am repelled by the embarrassments. Indeed, even the embarrassments are invitations to think more deeply and to work harder to allow worship to be the authentic celebrations God intends. I hope this volume may help reduce the embarrassments and extend the invitation of God's party.

But we must take seriously what it means to call worship God's party. How are we to understand and evaluate worship in the light of our faith in Jesus Christ? What is the meaning of Christian worship? To these questions we now turn.

2 Elephants in Church: Goals

A circus parade was moving gaily through the streets of Milan, Italy. Suddenly one of the elephants veered from the line and marched into a church. This visitor wandered up the center aisle, trumpeted a bit, swung her trunk around and headed back to the parade.

Unfortunately, many humans seem to imitate this pious pachyderm. On a Sunday morning we lurch into church, make a few noises, observe the congregation, then step out to resume our place in the parade. The great drama of worship is played out, but it is lost on us. We are elephants in church!

Man's capacity for worship is his distinguishing characteristic. It is this more than anything else which separates him from the animals. Elephants may be the objects of worship, as in some sects in India, but they may never be subjects in worship. Elephants may be revered. They cannot be reverent.

The sense of the sacred is unique with man as far as we know but this sensitivity is not easily developed. It comes very much as the sense of dramatic action comes to one learning the theater. A great deal of trouble is likely to develop in the church when certain fundamentals are not observed at the beginning. For this discussion, the following definitions are basic.

Elephants in Church: Goals

—Worship is the celebration of that which is of worth.

—Christian worship is the celebration of the gospel of Jesus Christ because Christians regard this gospel of supreme worth.[1]

—Liturgy is the work of the people in which the large drama of Christian worship is brought into focus, acted out in community, and rehearsed for further action in the world.

Quest for Meaningful Worship

There is much discussion and considerable controversy today about "contemporary worship." There are heated debates between those who argue for a "traditional" approach and those who want to be more "creative." The debate is an important one, although it is not always clearly focused or fruitful; and we shall try to enter into this major matter as we proceed. However, it is my conviction that the fundamental problem with worship today lies not with the adjective, but with the noun. What is *worship*? Until we have some clarity about the noun it is fruitless to argue about the adjective. What we need is worship, genuine Christian worship. Whether the materials of this worship are drawn from old sources or new is an important but secondary consideration.

The adjective that we will be using throughout this discussion is "meaningful." This word is chosen because it highlights the salient features of the noun "worship" and because it provides a link with the necessary but somewhat more abstract discussion of reality and language with which we must deal.

The quest for meaning is at the heart of contemporary worship. This is true for Roman Catholics for whom the revitalization of worship is nothing less than phenomenal. C. J. McNaspy emphasizes this in his comments on Pope Paul's interpretation of the Constitution on the Sacred Liturgy: "The Holy Father went on to

41

make clear that certain liturgical laws of the past are today inadequate. Accordingly, the Church is courageously trying to bring out the true meaning of liturgy, to deepen its social implications, to stress the worship function of the Word of God as presented in Holy Scripture and the homily."[2]

Donald Macleod, writing out of the Presbyterian tradition, takes a similar approach:

> The search for meaning, then, is the handle by which the contemporary revival of interest in worship is to be grasped and the most useful direction of this new concern determined. This is crucial because it has to do with even the *raison d'etre* of the Church itself. The Church's mission is to the whole man; and the crowning expression of it will be in the response it receives from the call, "I appeal to you therefore, brethren, by the mercies of God, to present your bodies as a living sacrifice, holy and acceptable to God, which is your spiritual worship." Such worship is concerned with every aspect of man's being, and hence the Church today faces here a compelling challenge which it must neither miss nor fail. Only as the Church inserts meaning into its worship and thereby projects or supplies a structure and framework for our common life can it hope to make men realize the peace and power of God as living realities.[3]

The issue is sharpened as we deal with new ways of worship. As the Lutheran scholar, Henry E. Horn, puts it: "Evaluation of new materials and forms is quite impossible until we have reestablished meaning for Christian worship."[4]

The meaning of "meaning" is complex, as C. K. Ogden and I. A. Richards have exhaustively stated. [5] By meaning in worship, as we are using the term here, we refer to worship that has a theological basis; that makes sense personally; that adds up socially; that opens up possibilities and has consequences for individuals, the church, and society.

First, on the way to meaning in worship, we must recover that sensitivity to the sacred which will keep us from becoming elephants in church. We cease being elephants in church when we understand what the *goals* of Christian worship are. One source of this understanding is the teaching of Jesus himself in his encounter with a lawyer, as recorded in Matthew 22:36-40. The lawyer was a Pharisee who qualified as a leader of worship in the synagogue. Yet Jesus had seen the vanity of much of that worship and had set about correcting it. He cleansed the temple and denounced the scribes and the Pharisees who had allowed worship to become a jumble of regulations that obscured "the weightier matters" of love and justice.

This passage recounts a crucial exchange between Jesus and the Pharisees, and while it does not deal specifically with worship, the word of Jesus actually offers the nerve center of a liturgy that is alive. "And one of them, a lawyer, asked, ... 'Teacher, which is the great commandment in the law?' And he said to him, 'You shall love the Lord your God with all your heart, and with all your soul, and with all your mind. This is the great and first commandment. And a second is like it, You shall love your neighbor as yourself. On these two commandments depend all the law and the prophets' " (RSV). Men cease to behave like elephants and become worshipers "in reality" when their worship provides an illuminating and empowering perspective on themselves, their neighbors, and God. This may seem to reverse the order of the text but, in both cases, God is regarded as supreme, and for modern man it is the problem of self which stands at the threshold of every endeavor.

Who Are We?

Worship tells us what nothing or no one else can: Worship tells us who we are. Arthur Miller's play *Death of a Salesman* stands as a definitive drama of our time because it tells of a man who was "just a little boat

43

looking for a harbor." Willy Loman at last takes his life because nobody ever told him who he was.

All around us are signs of the need for someone or something to tell us who we are. Cameras, mirrors, tape recordings are all signs of our need to affirm our existence to ourselves and to others.

We may long for a moment to see ourselves as others view us. Yet if that wish were granted it would surely be disillusioning. People are quick to pin labels upon us —too quick. They quickly dub us "fat" or "thin," we are either "conservative" or "liberal," we are either "a good old boy" or "an outsider." We play out our own kind of tragedy until we realize, as Willy Loman did not, that nobody can ever tell us who we are.

God knows us and in worship tells us who we are. The labels easily attached in daily life are torn off when we enter a service of genuine worship. Here we are no longer "fat" or "thin" or "liberal" or "conservative" or anything else, we are human beings "for whom Christ died" (I Corinthians 8:11). We know ourselves to be persons of worth because we are loved by God. This brings us a peace that the world cannot take away because the world did not give it to us.

Who Is Our Neighbor?

It is significant that Luke's version of our text uses the encounter of Jesus and the lawyer as the introduction to the parable of the Good Samaritan (Luke 10:25-37). Whittaker Chambers was right when he observed, "Men may seek God alone. They must worship him in common."

An American Indian parable tells of a hunter who saw in the distance what he thought was a beast. The hunter reached for an arrow. As the "beast" proceeded down the hill the hunter saw it was indeed a man, but he took him for an enemy. He placed the arrow in the bow. As he aimed he could see that the stranger was not his enemy but his brother. He dropped his bow and arrow and embraced him.

Genuine Christian worship is the occasion when our gaze pierces the illusion of the beastly and the hostile to perceive our brother. It is a time of loosening our grip on resentment and hostility to recognize our brother who is also one "for whom Christ died."

Who Is God?

At the end of a poem by Robert Louis Stevenson these lines appear:

> A stately music,
> Enter God.

The acid test of worship is whether after all the "stately music" there comes the "enter God." An amateur master of ceremonies presided at a banquet for the governor of his state. In the midst of his introduction the emcee became so flustered that he unwittingly adjourned the meeting. The governor was literally speechless. A minister may pride himself on his eloquence but unless he lets God speak, he is still the flustered amateur.

The questions some people ask after church are not the most appropriate ones. The question is not, Did I like the sermon? or, Did I enjoy the choir? J. C. Stewart suggests that the only question is, Did I or did I not meet Jesus Christ today? If that meeting does not take place, it doesn't matter whom else we meet at church. But when that meeting does take place in worship, it is likely to issue in a continuing conversation with the Christ throughout the week. Worship is a celebration of who God is and what he is doing in the world.

Celebration is itself a word that is now both popular and controversial. The word is popular, I think, because celebration carries with it that note of joy and triumph which is an integral part of the church's worship. The word is controversial, however, because for some people it seems to suggest a superficial joyfulness that does not take into effect the tragic dimensions of life. As I have been asked more than once, How do you tell a person who has just lost her husband to come to church and celebrate? Certainly celebration is not intended in any frivolous way that does not take seriously people's hurts; celebration in the original and still truest sense never suggests such frivolity. In fact, the original meaning carried with it the weight of a solemn gathering. To celebrate is to make public that joy which comes from worshiping God even in the midst of suffering and death. Celebration does not create a problem as long as it is God of the Christian revelation who is being celebrated.

The love of self, neighbor, and God that is awakened in genuine Christian worship is a continuous process. Each aspect of the love is integrally related to the other. On this basis, we can say then that the goals of Christian worship are:

—Recognition of ourselves as persons loved by God.

—Confrontation with our neighbor as one who needs us and one whom we need.

—Celebration of who God is and what he is doing in the world.

In stressing the goals of worship, as understood above, we are taking a somewhat different direction from that suggested by those who stress the *elements* of worship, or the basic *pattern* of worship. It is common, for example, for persons dealing with worship to take a passage such as Isaiah 6 and to suggest that herein is the pattern for all worship. The sequence of Isaiah's experience in the Temple becomes the pattern for all worship, moving variously through adoration, confession, supplication, and commitment. There are various interpretations of this. Not for one moment would I wish to detract from the beauty and power of this experience, or from its implications of our worship. However, there are serious questions whether this Temple experience is representative of the whole sweep of biblical faith, whether it shows the impact of Christ sufficiently, and whether it embraces the corporate dimension of worship that is so essential.

Where approaches that seek to find elements and patterns common to worship are used, I would still suggest that they be tested against this dynamic understanding of worship drawn from Jesus' own test of the adequacy of love. After all, what matters most is not whether certain elements are present, like bricks in a building, but whether the event of love is happening in our midst.

3 Criteria of Meaningful Worship

The first step toward meaningful worship is a clear understanding of its goals. These goals or purposes we have suggested are fundamentally the recognition of ourselves as loved by God, the confrontation with our neighbor as one who needs us and the celebration of who God is and what he is doing in the world.

These goals do not help us very much, however, unless they are linked with criteria that help us discriminate between materials and styles of worship that either help us or hinder us in reaching them. Criteria are simply standards on which a judgment or decision is based and thus they are consciously or unconsciously operative every time a service of worship is prepared, from the selection of hymns to the pronouncement of the benediction.

Stating criteria, or even following them, does not create worship. Worship is always a gift of God. On the other hand, if we don't try to express our preferences, set standards and clarify them, we are at the mercy of our opinions and the confines of our own experience. Unfortunately, a great deal of public worship suffers under a handicap of custom without conscious criteria. What James Reston said of the celebration of our Lord's resurrection is true of worship generally, "We have kept the parade but missed the Easter." Worship can be genuinely meaningful only when the criteria that guide us are valid and functional.

The quest for criteria for worship is ecumenical. The Constitution on the Sacred Liturgy which came from the Second Vatican Council is a major expression of this. Other studies (such as those of Hoon, MacLeod, Horn, and others, referred to throughout) share this same concern.

The United Methodist Church has been helped in this regard by the development of doctrinal guidelines.

Part of the genius of this statement to me is that it is at once confessional and ecumenical. Proceeding through the channels of one denomination it is nonetheless critically open to other streams and influences.

The Book of Discipline, 1972, sets forth these guidelines:

> Since "our present existing and established standards of doctrine" cited in the first two Restrictive Rules of the Constitution of The United Methodist Church are not to be construed literally and juridically, then by what methods can our doctrinal reflection and construction be most fruitful and fulfilling? The answer comes in terms of our free inquiry within the boundaries defined by four main sources and guidelines for Christian theology: Scripture, tradition, experience, reason. These four are interdependent; none can be defined unambiguously. They allow for, indeed they positively encourage, variety in United Methodist theologizing. Jointly, they have provided a broad and stable context for reflection and formulation. Interpreted with appropriate flexibility and self-discipline, they may instruct us as we carry forward our never-ending tasks of theologizing in The United Methodist Church.[1]

The question still remains as to how doctrinal guidelines actually guide our worship. To this question we turn.

Scripture

Christian worship should be biblically based.[2] The substance of Christian worship should be biblical. This principle is today shared by Roman Catholic and Protestant alike. This substance should reflect the whole of the Bible and not just select portions of it. Moreover, worship should be representative of the whole of biblical faith—the faith of the Bible, critically and prayerfully understood. Worship is not biblical, however, when it simply quotes the Bible. Worship is wholly biblical when the God who spoke through the Bible speaks again. Extensive studies in the sophisticated field of hermeneutics have opened up a deeper understanding of how we may listen to the Scriptures so that we discover not only what the text meant but what it means.[3]

Further, worship that is biblically based takes the Bible not only as its substance and the God of the Bible as its center, but the style of the Bible as its guide. Certainly there are many different literary genres in the Scriptures but the whole is marked by a language that is at once poetic and earthy. S. N. Behrman has described this in speaking of a contemporary novel:

> A word about the style which struck me: In its simplicity and emotional intensity it is Biblical. Stavros' family is deeply religious in the Christian tradition; they speak sparingly but everything they say glows with feeling. There is scarcely a word in this text that is not irradiated with emotion, primitive in the beginning and more complex after the young hero begins his wandering. But, throughout, the actual words that the characters say seem to be distilled like a sharp liquor from subterranean streams of harsh experience and hidden pools of desire . . . . The boy Stavros is rent by two homesicknesses; for the home he has abandoned, for the home he seeks. It is the pain in the heart of every migration. But there is a high exaltation, too. Stavros makes it.[4]

The language of worship (of which we shall say more later) should be biblical in this way even when it is not quoting the Bible. Then it is more likely that the God who spoke through the Bible will speak again. One way that this can be aided is to have readings from the Scriptures of a topical nature which draw together various biblical strands. For example, John J. Shaffer has prepared a responsive reading that draws together scriptural teachings on war and peace.[5] Another way in which the congregations may enter more fully into the biblical dimension is through a responsive prayer-scripture reading such as those developed by Kathryn Rogers Deering.[6] In this style the response of the congregation seeks to express how we might feel and react to the scriptural portion of the reading.

Frank Wood has used a similar approach to a litany based on Psalm 8.[7] Here the scripture is interlaced with honest contemporary reactions to the ancient word. Although at times this seems rather abrupt, the overall impact is much like the confessional tone of the Psalms themselves.

This question must be asked as we develop our liturgy, "Is this biblical in style as well as substance?"

Tradition

Christian worship should be historically conscious.[8] The church would seem to have little in common with McSorley's Ale House. However, a sign in the window of that famous institution, which has been a landmark in New York for generations, offers the clue, "We were here before you were born." Even ale houses have their traditions and they can be almost impregnable, as women's lib advocates discovered when they tried to infiltrate McSorley's. Such institutions can be changed, as the women proved, but only when there is a profound sense of how traditions develop.

The church was here before we were born. Only as we are conscious of what its history means are we free to help shape its future. We must be conscious of our past, or we will be imprisoned by it. A short view of history is one of the biggest detriments to genuine worship. What some people claim is "the way it has always been done" is as a matter of fact simply the way they remember it in their relatively short lifetimes. One way to break out of this prison is through cultivating an awareness of the long history of the church. There are, in fact, histories, and we must choose among them. This we cannot do until we become deliberately conscious about our past.

We need to become historically conscious, moreover, because otherwise we cannot understand what it means to be Christian. The creeds we affirm, the hymns we sing, to say nothing of the scriptures we interpret, may create a new future for us, but they come to us out of the past. Without a sensitivity to the dedicated minds and devoted hearts of our fathers, we cannot understand where we are.

More deeply to remember, to recollect, is to plumb the depths of our life and faith. From the time of Israel onward the worshiping community has affirmed that the God of our fathers is our God also. There are depths in our collective unconscious, to use Carl Jung's phrase, that reverberate with meanings.

To be historically conscious is to affirm the years. Christian worship is not an enemy to time. History is not an illusion. Time is not a shadow for Christian faith. That men come and go while God remains faithful is at the heart of our Christian affirmation. To be conscious of our history is to recognize the God who is at once within time and yet beyond time, to recognize our mortality and God's immortality.

To be historically conscious is not only to be free for the future but to find resources for the future. Some of the most "contemporary" materials for an insight into worship come from past eras that we are only beginning to appreciate today. For example, one of the most contemporary services of Holy Communion (that is, one of the services most consistent with the modern temper in its economy and directness) is also one of the oldest services of Communion, that of Hippolytus. The inherent quality of much of what has been produced in the past survives the test of time.

We ask of our materials for worship, "Does this express the faith of our fathers? And if it does not do so directly, how is this related to that faith?''

Experience

Christian worship should be personally and corporately authentic.[9] However difficult it is to pinpoint and however difficult to achieve, we must face the fact that the persons who worship must find that which is real to them. The service of worship should be like a mirror held up to the congregation. They should see who they are in order to realize who they may become. The shock of recognition should pulse through worship. Hearing the prayer, listening to the sermon, the worshiper should feel, "That's me!" Simple as this sounds, a great deal of worship fails at this point. People sit numbly in their pews and after a while simply leave because, reading prayers and listening to sermons, they have the feeling that whoever prepared these materials has no idea of who they are, of who their neighbor is, of what their life is like, or "where it's at" for them.

The problem is partly that of language, of which we shall say more later. We tend to spend much time in liturgy with a language that we use nowhere else, and this reduces the connection between our worship and our daily life.

There needs also to be more genuine emotion in our worship. For many people, perhaps most, the deepest problems of their life are not so much with what they think, but how they feel. Love, hate, fear, hope—these are emotions, and they must be dealt with in worship. To be sure, we must avoid an excessive emotionalism that plays on feelings in the most superficial way, but we cannot avoid the realities of emotion if we are to have a genuine worship. Music, theater games, sensitivity exercises, and creative movement are ways to let the depths of emotion find expression. As such, they are not entertainment items to be added to an emotionally sterile service. Such means of expression are the essence of genuine worship.

But above all, there should be that awareness that this service of worship is our service of worship. To the greatest degree possible, the worshiper should participate in the preparation of the service. Even where this is not directly possible, those who do prepare the service should be so immersed in the life of the congregation that the worshipers identify with the service.

The question is important: Is this, our worship of God, enriching our lives?

Reason

Worship should be theologically discerning.[10] The God who is being celebrated is none other than the God of the Christian revelation. To discern this is to engage in that exercise of reason called theology which is basic to worship.

Worship as the celebration of that which is of worth is a broadly human activity not specifically Christian. One social commentator has observed that the huge shopping centers often located in our suburbs are theological institutions. He shrewdly sees that how people spend their money tends to locate their gods and express their values. Our daily speech betrays the same tendency. We speak of someone who "worships" his lawn, for example, or we "idolize" a film star.

Popular entertainment is an arena where our worship activity is most conspicuous. Recently I attended a pop concert with my children and was awed by its "religious" character. The concert was held in a building very much like a temple; the devotees were there in the hundreds; the master of ceremonies, priestlike, guided the initiates through the service. Chants of approval arose when numbers were completed by the preliminary performers. Then the star appeared. Here was the one they had been waiting for—a kind of mod messiah. I strained to hear the message of deliverance he would bring. Yes, that's what he was saying, "La -la, la, la -la, la, la -la, la, la." Somehow he was able to make that profound statement sound like an answer to prayer. The crowd was overwhelmed; dozens poured forward just to touch the fringe of his garment. The offering was not so much presented to as showered upon the performer. Objects of adoration were flung at him throughout his act, and at the end the stage was covered with tribute that included programs, beads, rings, bubblegum, candy, and bread. But when the lights went on he was gone, and there was a chilling emptiness about the place.

This had been an experience of worship in the sense that people were celebrating something that was of worth to them, at least for a while. The elements of ritual were everywhere, but it was not an act of Christian worship because the "god" who was being worshiped was not the God of the Christian revelation. The love that was being extolled was not that of God's pouring forth of himself for men, and there was no concern expressed for one's brother.

That such "worship" is idolatrous is easily seen. What is far more difficult to discern are the more subtle ways in which people worship Mars, the god of war, or the nation state, or the American way of life. Such idols very easily make their way into the sanctuary of the church. For this reason Christian worship must be theologically discerning. It must penetrate the "gods of our time" and expose the idols of the moment for what they are. Theological perception, which enables us to make this distinction in the preparation of worship, is not a nice refinement, it is an utter necessity.

As a congregation looks at every aspect of its worship, theological discernment is essential. It is especially crucial as the congregation seeks to develop the affirmation of its faith. Deane Postlethwaite has prepared suggestions by means of which his congregation developed affirmations of faith. He writes:

It is hoped that the creed will be:
1. Prepared only after serious attention has been given to the *sources of faith* such as:
   a. The Bible
   b. The historic creeds and church tradition—that is "what has been handed down."
   c. Contemporary creeds and creedal statements, especially those coming from:
      (1) Ecumenical sources.
      (2) Protestantism, Methodism, and our local church.
      (3) All individuals participating in the creed-writing experience.
2. A personal statement, as honest and explicit as possible, but one that is to be used in corporate worship, that is a document of a community of faith, that could properly begin, "We believe."
3. A statement that comes after attention has been given to the various categories of traditional creeds, that is God, the Church, etc. If certain categories are omitted it should be by conscious judgment.
4. A statement in modern language and thought patterns showing concern for style, balance and beauty of expression.[11]

In addition to these four guidelines directly from the doctrine and doctrinal statements of The United Methodist Church, there are at least two more that should be added as criteria for worship. The concern for mission that is implicit in the four guidelines becomes explicit in the materials developed in contemporary worship. I believe it is valid and consistent with the other guidelines. The other additional criterion—that of liturgical wholeness—is basically an aesthetic consideration and has to do with the integrity and overall design of the service as a whole.

Sensitivity to Mission

Christian worship should be sensitively missional. Christian worship should help us discern the God who is moving in our time and calling us to create a new history under the Lordship of Christ.

Criteria of Meaningful Worship

A boy in Wisconsin was reading about the human heart and how it works. Fascinated by the book, he decided to test its theory, and he put his ear to the chest of his little brother. What he heard was not the kind of sound he had been taught to expect. He called to his mother and she, too, listened to a strange, squishy noise in place of the normal heartbeat. The mother became alarmed and took the little fellow to the doctor. It was discovered that he was in urgent need of heart surgery, which he promptly got. Christian worship should be like that experience. It should be a time when we listen to our brother's heart. It should be the occasion when, figuratively, we put our ear close to our brother so that we can hear the pain and the hope, the anguish and the possibilities in his life.

Worship that merely catalogs heart failures, however, is not truly Christian worship. That is, liturgy that simply recites aspects of a human tragedy is as faulty as liturgy that seeks to ignore them. What is called for is the creative approach, which sees in the troubled situations of the world an opportunity to serve one's brother. Genuinely missional worship is distinguished from immature and irresponsible social commentary precisely in the way in which it opens up opportunities for the people of God to accept responsibility for the world. Genuine Christian worship has an acute sense of time and place. It is the worship of a particular congregation at a particular time and place with particular responsibilities laid upon it. It will do no one any good if he has loved God in general and hated his neighbor next door. That church which has not found the connection between its liturgy and its mission has yet to discover the meaning of worship.

Sometimes this missional dimension is expressed in a specific act in worship. For example in Otterbein United Methodist Church Pastor David Harris was dealing with the issues of war and peace. As part of the service of worship postcards were passed out and people were encouraged to write to a prisoner of war. The sharing of concerns is another way in which many congregations bring this missional dimension to expression, although this falls short if it is merely cataloging of current events unaccompanied by action or the will to act.

One of the most important ways of expressing the missional element is through the structure of the service itself. The gathering-scattering structure, such as is found in many of the new profiles of worship, is much more missional in its orientation than some older patterns, which focused all the congregation's concerns inwardly. In these new profiles of worship the going-forth of the congregation to serve in the world is what worship is about.

We ask as we prepare the service of worship, Does this help us be sensitive to our neighbor and reach out to extend the mission of our church?

Liturgical Wholeness

Christian worship should be liturgically whole. The elements of a service of worship should come together in a unified and unifying pattern.

This unity may be more like that of a profile of a face than a menu on which items are listed in specific categories. That is, the unity may be found in the overall impression of the service rather than in the mechanical order imposed upon it. But there should be a basic intentionality that pulses through the whole service and relates the elements of the service to a common direction for the life of the congregation.

This central intention or basic theme of the service is necessary. Without it we may have simply a collection of items with no inner coherence. But this unity is necessary not only for rational and aesthetic factors in the abstract but also because, if the meaning of the worship is to be carried out into the life of the people, it must be simple enough to be grasped. Perhaps not every line or every aspect of the service will be equally related to the center, but if a common intentionality moves through the whole, then, if it is picked up at any point, it will move in the direction of the service of God.

Thus the question, How does this element of worship key in to the basic intentionality or major theme of the service? How does it relate to the other elements in the service in terms of theme and style?

Unity does not mean the end of diversity. Rather, it is simply the framework in which true variety can be expressed. There should always be a balance between the familiar and the unfamiliar.

One way of achieving this is through "annotations or directions" in the outline of the service. That is, for example, elements that may be closer together are annotated thus: "the congregation gathers to hear the Word of God." Familiar elements may be given a new direction by such an annotation. Likewise, unfamiliar elements may be set in context by this simple but increasingly popular method.

Again, let it be said that stating the criteria or meeting them does not in itself guarantee genuine worship, but it does tend to make us better prepared to receive that genuine worship which is the gift of God. It keeps us from being victimized by our own personal prejudices and opens the way toward a more communal worship by trying to raise the criteria of worship to that conscious level at which they can be discussed, clarified, and negotiated between persons.

Our concern in this section has been to deal with criteria for liturgy. However, we should recall that liturgy is the sharp communal focus of the drama of worship that is being played out every day. Not all that is signaled in the criteria will be found in a particular service nor perhaps in many services taken together. The point is that liturgy opens into life, indeed is an intensification of life and of the ongoing work of the people of God. We assume a community of persons who are not only worshiping together but helping administer the life of a congregation, dealing with Christian education, providing opportunities for counseling and social action. Thus, for example, the task of personal authenticity would not necessarily mean that everyone's emotional problems are dealt with in depth in the service of worship itself. Personal authenticity in worship, however, should mean that the door is left open for dealing with emotional realities through groups or counseling once they've been recognized as being real in the service of worship.

Christian worship should be biblically based, historically conscious, personally and corporately authentic, theologically discerning, sensitively missional, and liturgically whole. These are the criteria by which the elements of a service of worship and the total are judged.

Stated in the form of questions that persons may ask as they consider each element in the service and all the elements together, these criteria may be expressed as follows:

1. Is this material biblical in style, as well as substance?
2. Does this express the faith of our fathers, and if it does not do so directly, how is it related to that faith?
3. Is this our worship of God enriching our lives and genuinely involving the whole congregation?
4. Does this focus our worship on the God of the Christian revelation?
5. Does this help us be sensitive to our neighbor and reach out to extend the mission of our Church?
6. How does this element of worship key in to the basic intention or major theme of the service and relate to its overall style?

Liturgy should open into life. That it often does not is a problem that we must now explore more fully.

4 Reality and Language

Sleeping in Church: The Real Issue

The basic problem for worship is that the reality of liturgy and the reality of daily life no longer come together. Often what transpires in church is so remote from what goes on in daily life that there seems to be no connection between the two.[1] And sometimes when a connection is attempted, it is so tentative or faulty that it fails to convince us that there is genuine relationship between liturgy and life.

One result of this is absence. Many people simply stay away from church because it makes no difference to their lives. Another result is sleep. Most preachers would probably be shocked if they knew how few people listen to what they are saying. One art of which laymen quickly become masters is that of going to sleep with their eyes open. For children who are brought by their parents, this is a bit more difficult, as is evidenced in a conversation that took place between a certain ten-year-old boy and his father on their way home on the first Sunday that the boy went to sleep in church.

Son: Well, Dad, now I'm just like you. I've gone to sleep in church.

Father: Did you really go to sleep?

Son: Yeah, and I got a good rest last night, too.

Pause.

Father: Let's try to figure out why you went to sleep.

Son: Okay.

Father: I think you went to sleep because what was going on in church had nothing to do with your life.

Son: Yeah. The music was like an opera, and I don't like opera with people going like (here came a youthful imitation of operatic singing). I don't understand it. Like that's the *past*.

Father: Yes, it's more like saving the past than making a future. Yet, in the past, worship at its best was close to life, in the home, in the streets and restaurants: like Jesus.

Worship that is primarily the preservation of the past fails to do justice even to the past and will do little to relate to the present.

Another result of the rift with reality is hypocrisy. One of the loudest and most damning indictments of the church today is that it engages in hypocrisy. On Sunday, people gather to mouth high-sounding platitudes that are promptly contradicted by their behavior as soon as they set foot outside the church. Naturally, there are many people who continue to come to church who feel this insidious threat gnawing away at them. They test the gap between their high ambitions and lower conduct. But instead of feeling truly humble or penitent, they simply feel guilty and, after a while, they give up altogether.

Certainly, there can be no lowering of the high standards of moral and ethical conduct to which the Christian faith calls us. Likewise, much of our guilt is justified because we have not had the resolution and the discipline to do what we should.

But a large part of our problem rests not only with our resolution but with our understanding of the real. We virtually pledge ourselves to a hypocritical existence because the way we understand reality creates a split at the very heart of our lives. Tragically, we tend to locate our faith in a "spiritual" realm that has little or no contact with the realities of our daily lives.

Let us be clear at the beginning of this discussion that there is a fundamental sense in which the reality of a God who is worshiped and the reality of daily life do not coincide. God is God, and man is man. It is not necessary to accept uncritically the Kierkegaardian understanding of God as "the wholly Other," although this may be both true and helpful.

What we are talking about here is the Creator/creature distinction that is so fundamental from Genesis through Romans and, indeed, beyond. That God is the Creator who is transcendent above the creation and that we creatures are to worship him is utterly basic. Where this distinction is not observed and people at worship tend to treat God as if he were a pal or one of the boys reflects an illegitimate approach to the deity. God is God, and man is man. They meet in worship, but they do not merge organically.

This Creator/creature distinction is ill-served, however, when confused with Platonic metaphysics or linguistic oddity. The distinctiveness of God lies in his being God, not in his being addressed in seventeenth-century language or being preached about by men in medieval academic dress nor by having all this transpire in architectural styles from another age. As recognition of the historical dimensions of faith, all this may have its place. To confuse this with the otherness of God is to make a fatal mistake. To think that God's holiness must be protected by cultural archaisms is to admit precisely that what one is worshiping is not the God of the biblical revelation. God is nonetheless holy for being addressed as "you" rather than as "thou." Indeed, when "thou" was originally used it was the more personal rather than formal style of address. It is characteristic of contemporary worship to use "you" rather than "thou" in addressing God, so this more intimate form is actually a recovery of an old tradition in which God's transcendence is perceived in his immanence.

The point here is that the crucial distinction between God and man lies in their status, not in their reality. The real world of which God is Creator is the same real world in which I am his creature. The real world, over which God is transcendent, is the same real world in which God is immanent. Man's status in the world is distinct from God's but God and man are related. Reality is in the relationship.

We cannot get to the root of worship until we get to the root of reality. The matter is complicated because, although the understanding of reality here is older than the Old Testament, it has been obscured, I think, by a good deal of thought that has been extremely influential in shaping the worship we now experience. Therefore, it will be necessary for us to take a look at how we got where we are and to consider some of the options for today.

We should be encouraged in this discussion by remembering that, while the discussion may be at times abstract, it is nonetheless practical. Indeed, our practice cannot really be operative without dealing with these matters. Moreover, we may be sustained at least in part by the way in which one of our leading comics has perceived how fundamental this problem is as it relates to worship. Bill Cosby observes that there are two kinds of sneezes; there is the sneeze on the subway and the sneeze in church. On a subway, one sneezes with abandon, with gusto, and with volume. It is relief and it is enjoyable, at least for the one who sneezes. However, says Cosby, you will notice that people sneeze in church in an entirely different manner. They try to sniff it back, and when at last it forces its way, the person tries to choke it down and it may come out as a mild, eye-watering cough, restrained but without relief. In observing that there is one kind of sneeze delivered in a subway and another in church, Cosby has focused precisely on that rift in reality which is the subject of our inquiry.

What is real? It is an urgent question. One pop song recently declared that "nothing is real," we live in strawberry fields in which all is an illusion. The question is basic to our lives because we live in terms of what we believe to be real.

Reality is what we bump against. We discover reality by groping. It does not yield to our fancy but shapes us, instead. Reality is what we are ultimately up against.

To understand the forces in the modern world that actually shape our understanding of reality, we must come to grips with Friedrich Hegel.[2] Whereas Aristotle had worked largely on the basis of nature, Hegel took his clues from the study of history. Reality was that which manifested itself in the unfolding of the time span. His interpretation of history was that there is a dialectic in history in which a thesis is countered by an antithesis that gives rise to a synthesis.

In making this approach, Hegel made a direct attack on Aristotle, whom he believed had misunderstood the nature of reality. The process of thought that Aristotle followed did not allow for contradiction. It was not possible for something to be A and not be A at the same time. However, in history, in life around him, Hegel saw constant contradiction. His dialectic of thesis, antithesis, synthesis was a way of accounting for the contradictions of life. Hegel's system was less neat but more dynamic. It was closer to the processes of history.

In turn, Hegel was attacked by Sören Kierkegaard.[3] Kierkegaard felt that Hegel's schemes were too grandiose. He thought the broad generalizations of Hegel were fanciful and like the thoughts of a man who dreamed of a castle but was forced to live in a hut. The dialectic of life is more like the progress of a pilgrim who passes through stages along life's way from the aesthetic to the ethical to the religious A and religious B. Life moves as the self either wills to be itself or wills not to be itself. One can work out his salvation, albeit in fear and trembling.

Interestingly, Kierkegaard is the first one of the thinkers mentioned so far who was a clergyman and whose views issued in prolific prayers and sermons (though he later turned away from the institutional church of his day). This in itself, however, ought not to make us too kindly toward the Dane. In spite of his basic temperamental differences, he remains nonetheless indebted to Hegel, who had the genius to transpose back into the historical the categories that Plato and Aristotle had rendered naturalistically.

Still, it is Kierkegaard who becomes a key figure in the perception of reality. Kierkegaard sees the self, with its will and imagination, negotiating the crises of everyday life. However offensive this is to the mind that seeks careful categories, it is the way we experience history.

The fundamental insight and direction of Kierkegaard were taken up along with other streams of thought by a group of thinkers known as phenomenologists. Phenomenology, as developed by Edmund Husserl, Martin Heidegger, Jean-Paul Sartre, Merleau-Ponty and others, concentrates on that point of contact between the subject, who experiences, and the object of experience. Phenomenology is "a study of consciousness *as intentional*, as directed toward objects, as living in an intentionally constituted world."[4]

In the words of Karl Jaspers, "we call reality that which is present to us in practice, that which in our dealings with things, with living creatures, and with men is resistance or becomes matter. We learn to know reality through our daily association with people, through the handling of tools, through technical knowledge, through contact with organized bodies of men. . . . But by its very nature the knowledge of reality transcends the immediate interests of practical life."[5]

Reality is a structure of many levels through which there pulses intentionality. This is analogous to Kierkegaard's understanding of life as a movement of the self to fulfillment through the various stages.

Phenomenology offers the comprehensive understanding of reality that seems to be assumed in the Bible and is called for in our understanding of worship. It is no wonder, then, that some of the most profound and contemporary studies of worship proceed from a phenomenological base. (See the work of Marianne H. Micks and Ross Snyder.)[6] In the recognition of the multilayered structure of reality, we are saved from the artificial choice of reality as "thing" or reality as "abstraction." If reality is a multilayered structure, then it must embrace these dimensions and others as well.

Our complaint about the lack of reality in worship can now be seen as a complaint that the worship we have known has operated on only one level whereas we live our lives on many levels. But, if what we have said is correct, the problem is deeper than that. The problem is that reality has been seen as dealing with a few aspects of our existence, whereas reality deals with our existence in its wholeness. Much worship is as dull as getting in an elevator, watching the doors close, then getting out without going anywhere. Such worship has that dullness because it's that kind of experience. When we understand that reality operates on many levels, then we can stop at each floor, as it were, and gain something there. When we come out at a different level from where we went in, more enriched than we were before, then we are beginning to imagine some of the kinds of benefits that worship will bestow upon us when it reflects a more adequate and comprehensive understanding of reality.

Further, reality recurs. That is, the layers of reality are designated as such because, again and again, persons have found and are still finding these factors with which they must deal in their existence.

The key is the self in its imagining. By self, of course, I am referring not to an isolated ego but to the self in its relationships (see chapter 1). And by the imagination I mean "the will in its cognitive function" (Ray Hart) not fancy. Reality lies in the totality of the multi-layered structure. But the multi-layered structure is not perceived at any single moment.

What the self perceives at any given moment is the relationship or disrelationship between the elements of the structure. In a film by Ingmar Bergman, a character declares, "I must live in line with something I believe true." When the basic elements of our lives are "in line" the connection is struck that completes the circuit of meaning and provides illumination and power. This is the reality by which we live or die.

When the self sees the action of God and one's daily life in line with each other, insight takes place. It is the experience described by Gestalt psychology. Then the reality of God and the reality of our daily life come together in such a way as to create a new future.

When this happens in liturgy, life is on its way to becoming Christian worship.

This journey cannot be made without language. To the issue of language and liturgy we must now move.

Waking Up: Toward a New Language of Liturgy

The ten-year-old boy just awakened after going to sleep in church for the first time continued his conversation with his father. The boy remembered a scene from the Gospels he had heard about in a song and had seen represented in statuary. "The woman at the well: Jesus talked to her about life. This morning the preacher was just talking about words."[7]

Dietrich Bonhoeffer seemed like a man who had gone to sleep in some dull services himself and reached

Reality and Language

a similar conclusion. In his *Letters and Papers from Prison* there appears this passage which at once shocks us and thrills us with hope.

It is not for us to prophesy the day (though the day will come) when men will once more be called so to utter the word of God that the world will be changed and renewed by it. It will be a new language, perhaps quite non-religious, but liberating and redeeming —as was Jesus' language; it will shock people and yet overcome them by its power; it will be the language of a new righteousness and truth, proclaiming God's peace with men and the coming of his kingdom.[8]

Implied in this brief statement are at least two things. The first is that the "old" language, by which Bonhoeffer means the language inherited from the nineteenth century with its metaphysical underpinnings, is no longer potent. This is not to say that the nineteenth-century language is not beautiful or valuable to some. It is simply to say that it is no longer powerful. This is surely a commentary on us, as well as on our language—if we can even separate the two. But the truth is that we are men with broken tongues.

The second implication in this statement is that a new language is not yet present. The language is not present in the church. The problem is not that men hear the preacher and reject his claim—they often just do not hear the preacher. There are "words," of course; but they do not carry, they do not reverberate, they do not strike home. Nor is the language present in the world. It is not a matter of finding some vocabulary already operative and fitting Christian meanings to it; there is no such universal language today. We live in a time of broken tongues.

This appraisal is shocking, but it is also hopeful. It is, first of all, an honest word. This is where we are. Wherever this realistic assessment of our situation is present, we are liberated. We are freed from further kidding of ourselves. It is not now a task of getting a "sermon starter" from this periodical or a snappy prayer of confession from that magazine or a catchy picture from the *Daily News*. Our situation is much more grave. It is as if one whose problem has been walking around water on the deck was suddenly pitched into the sea. He thought his problem was how to avoid getting wet; instead, it is how to stay alive. To recognize the depth of our plight is the first step toward dealing with it.

Second, the assessment is hopeful because it means that we are responsible, each one of us. We are responsible for our language. Language is problematical, and it is now a problem—no one else will solve it for us, no one else can. Of course, we can parrot others if we choose; we can repeat the same slogans and avoid the dangerous words. But that is suicide. It is death to us and to the possibility that in the salty depths before we die our feet may kick the black oyster with one true and shining meaning in it. And this is a thrilling possibility: that shipwrecks like ourselves may utter a cry with life in it—that we may participate in the quest for the true intention. In the awful ache within us a new language is struggling to be born. We must give birth! Each one of us!

In such a time no serious attempt to understand language should be rejected. Even on a road that may turn into a dead end, we can learn something; and some attempts, while they do not resolve a basic problem, nevertheless are useful and sometimes necessary intermediate steps. For example, there were some who believed that the translation of the Latin Mass into English would resolve the problem of understanding what was going on. There is considerable evidence, however, that when the translation was made, what occurred was the contrary. The substitution of English words for Latin was satisfactory to very few. The enormous mystery of the ancient language seemed dissipated in a flat modernity almost immediately. "Folk masses" developed that brought the musical dimension into play. And, even here, as much controversy as clarity seems to have resulted. Another type of attempt is simply to attempt to substitute contemporary words for ancient words. This would make the mistake of thinking of faith as an object that only needed the labels changed. It was such an approach that drew scorn, for putting new wine in the old wineskins makes them burst.

What is fundamentally wrong with such approaches is that they still assume an uncritical acceptance of language as primarily "words." The word *language* comes from the Latin *lingua,* which means tongue. Language traditionally has meant the words, pronounciation and methods of combining them. But we are living in a time in which communications have expanded so enormously that this understanding of language is no longer workable. It is too limited, and it is too limiting. This is not to say that language as words, and particularly spoken words, is obsolete. It is simply to say that this can no longer be our exclusive understanding of language. As we shall see later on, spoken language continues to be the paradigm for language although it is no longer the complete range for language.

What is called for is a new understanding of language itself. In this search I believe that we may learn a great deal from persons who have helped us see a new understanding of reality because they have perceived that reality and language are intimately related.

Language and Reality. In the traditional view of language, words pointed to or conveyed "reality." In the phenomenological view, language too expresses reality. Or, as some put it, language brings reality to expression. The philosopher Martin Heidegger, for example, holds that "language is not a mere tool, one of the many which man possesses; on the contrary, it is only language that affords the very possibility of standing in the openness of the existent."[9] Language is the voice of reality, the call that brings us consciously into its presence.

The New Testament scholar, Ernst Fuchs, carries this understanding forward in his study of Jesus. Language, for Fuchs, is that which "makes being into an event.[10] Jesus demonstrated this understanding of language, Fuchs observes, when he said to the paralytic, "Arise and walk." These words were not simply command, they were promise. They created the situation in which they could be fulfilled.

This understanding of language and reality does not deny that language may be used to point or to convey information. In fact, a good deal of our day-to-day conversation is of that sort. But this approach denies that such a use of language is either exclusive or definitive. The definitive understanding of language here is that word is fully word when it is word event. Word event is word as it discloses reality, imparts power, opens a future, and sets men moving.

In this understanding of language what is communicated is not idea but intentionality. Intentionality is consciousness of and motion toward. It is the meaning that is communicated.

If language is the voice of reality, then the inadequacy of words immediately becomes obvious, as we have already seen in the preceding discussion. Reality is a multilayered structure. Words deal only with one, or perhaps several, of the layers.

The unconscious expresses itself through posture, gesture, movement, touch, and other nonverbal means. Kinesics is a developing science that seeks to decode the meanings of our "body language."[11]

Sound is the fundament of the multilayered structure of the work of art, as Ingarden pointed out. The groan or squeal is the beginning of the speech that may launch a love affair or a war.

The written word is an extension of speech. However obscure may be the connection between high art and lower levels of speech, it is there.

Sights communicate. The work of an artificer or an artist may tell us more about a scene than our optical vision of a place.

Images arise to give shape to our lives. As C. G. Jung so masterfully pointed out, images are not unreal shadows but "the wordless occurrences" called forth by life that need no substances. They are like symbols that spring from life and return to life in experience and in deed.

Emotions have a language that expresses itself through the senses. We touch someone—in anger or love—and change a situation.

The social world has an extensive vocabulary. What we hear emanates from another; what we say is to be heard by another.

Things communicate. The shape of the objects of our daily life tell of our life-style.

The environment speaks. E. T. Hall, the anthropologist, has written of the "silent language" by which a culture communicates its values and meanings.

Liturgy is to take place in reality, and if reality is a multilayered structure, then we need a liturgical language that expresses the fullness of reality. The words we say may be a small part of what is communicated. Some studies have attempted to show that only a small percentage of what is communicated is done so by our words. More is communicated by our tone of voice, posture, etc. Such studies are important, but they ought not to be overemphasized. Only a small portion of the space of the human body is taken up by the eyes, but without them we could not see. Likewise, although words, as such, occupy a small "space," they are the sources by which much light is let into the house of language. What is needed is not a denial of the word, but an understanding that awakens the eventfulness of words; and this will mean an extension of language. For example, architecture, instead of being thought of as merely the "setting" for worship, must be seen as part of the language of worship itself.[12]

The movement of the body in worship must mean more than simply getting up and sitting down, for movement is expressive. It is virtually impossible to worship without movement. The question is only whether the movement will be intentional, expressive, and offered up in praise of God, or simply ignored. Standing to sing, kneeling or bowing to pray, are only some of the gestures that make our worship more meaningful.

Symbolic movement or interpretative dance is the epitome of movement. A trained dancer or choreographer can show a large congregation how to express its praise of God through movement. An interpretative choir can express the meaning of a song or a passage of scripture in ways that sum up depths of meaning. A skilled dancer can draw from a text meanings that are hidden by other modes of interpretation.

Dance is one of the hallmarks of the new forms of worship. Sometimes this dance expresses itself amid folk and rock music, banners, and balloons with everyone dancing. Marge Champion has recently attracted a good deal of attention for her dance in the church.[13] Thom Jones, a minister and a dancer of distinction now with the United Methodist Board of Discipleship, is actively awakening creative movement in worship.

The way in which dance can interpret faith is shown in a powerful and graceful dance of the Apostles' Creed choreographed by Gemze de Lappe and Buzz Miller and featuring Lyn Seymour of the Royal Ballet.[14] This creed, which is recited every Sunday all around the world, is a profound and passionate statement about who we are as persons in relation to the ultimate forces in the universe; in relation to the heroic challenges of life; in relation to the communion of persons in all ages. But the creed is an ice cube for many people—cold and square. We recite it, but we don't believe it, let alone like it. In *Credo* the dancers move across the frozen creed and melt its crust so that its vital force can flow again. The believer is depicted as a traveler along the way. God the Father appears as a protective and supportive figure who is not literally seen by the believer. In the second article of the creed the Son appears as one who carries a bundle quite like that of the burden carried by the believer. In the third movement the Holy Spirit lifts the traveler up to assume the cruciform shape of the Lord. *Credo* is a superb example of the way in which dance can liberate meaning and illuminate faith and life.

New music is another hallmark of the developing ways of worship. The hymnody that we have inherited has been rich, often pleasant, and sometimes stirring to many people. It has also been restricted to a narrow range of musical forms, with a heavy tendency toward pastoral and military language in the lyrics. The new music is bursting out of these old forms and striking out in many fresh directions. Songs such as "They Will Know We Are Christians by Our Love," by Peter Scholtes; "Allelu!" and "Clap Your Hands," by Ray Repp; and "Gonna Sing, My Lord," by Joe Wise come immediately to mind. These works are largely in the tradition of folk music and have brought warmth and spontaneity to worship.

Ed Summerlin, who was among the first to use jazz liturgically, has included music with a heavy rock beat, electronic music, and the synthesizer in a highly creative way. With Roger Ortmayer he has written songs such as "Hello, Goodby" that definitely enlarge the range of our hymnody toward a joyful contemporariness.

Floyd E. Werle has also used the synthesizer and a wide range of musical styles in developing new music for worship. He has, for example, done a version of "Joyful, Joyful, We Adore Thee" to a fast twist beat. The hymns of Phil West are worthy of note because of their heavy contemporary urban imagery, which carries a punch that is not always felt in music that grows out of the folk tradition.

By no means is all the new music for the church being written expressly for that purpose. Some of the most powerful of the new hymns and songs are coming from so-called secular sources. There is an undeniably prophetic note in much of the work of Bob Dylan. There is a deep pervasive spirituality moving through many of the Beatle songs, including "Let It Be" and a powerful vision of Christ emerges in Janice Ian's "New Christ Cardiac Hero."

This new music is not to be seen merely as a "jazzing up" of old pieties. The new music is nothing less than a challenge to the old language of worship and a deliberate and massive development of a new form of liturgical language.[15]

The same may be said of multi-media in general. Specifically, portable video has created a new arena for the audio-visual. I have employed video in worship by taping key events of the General Assembly of the National Council of Churches as they occurred, editing, and then projecting the images as part of the service recollecting the week. Video has an infinite variety of uses and is especially valuable for helping persons see who they are and how they relate. With the coming of cable television new possibilities are opening to us.

The church year is part of the new liturgical language as of the old. We might say that the church year is the tense over which the syntax of the new language is spelled out. The seasons and colors of the church year are familiar: Advent, purple; Christmastide, white; Epiphany, white; Lent, purple; Good Friday, black; Eastertide, white; Pentecost, red; and Kingdomtide, green are the traditional pattern of United Methodist worship. However, the meaning of the church year goes deeper than the changing of colors, as Marianne Micks points out so brilliantly in her work. The title tells it: the Christian sense of time in the church year is a way of making "the future present." Two studies dealing with the Christian year are especially worthy of note. One is the *Christian Year and Lectionary Reform*, by A. Allen MacArthur.[16] This excellent reconstruction of the lectionary proposes a reform that does more justice to the trinitarian nature of our faith than do many of the traditional lectionaries. MacArthur proposes a season of God the Father, a season of God the Son, and a season of God the Holy Spirit. Keith Watkins' book *Liturgies in a Time When Cities Burn*[17] has an excellent chapter, "Weekend and Holy Day," that suggests a pattern by which the seasons of the church year should come together with the holiday pattern of our national life in a creative way. There is in this connection an enormous potential that has hardly begun to be developed. Spelling it out could be a major adventure in our liturgical life.

For an attempt to render this understanding of a language of liturgy in outline, see pages 78 and 79.

What is being suggested here is an attempt to establish some foundations for the development of a new language for liturgy. There is no intention to offer a scheme for a foolproof universe of discourse or to create some theological equivalent of Esperanto—an ersatz language for all purposes. The aim is quite different: simply to discern the foundations and guidelines around which an authentic language seems most likely to appear.

Even such a modest aim as this may meet with objections from at least two sources. One is that group which holds that language is a gift of creative inspiration and simply cannot be worked at. It is reported that Edgar Allan Poe's reputation as an author was seriously hampered when he published his *Philosophy of Composition*, which made clear how he labored over his writing. The public wanted to believe that his work was a gift of the muses. Well, Poe's work was a gift, but it was *his* gift and the muses had little to do with it. There may seem to be the exception of a few hours of genius here and there, but even these hours invariably presuppose long days and nights of meditation and years of discipline. Ernest Hemingway was a creative writer if there ever was one. But read about his tortures of trying to get just one true

77

Elements of Liturgical Language

Nonverbal	Literal	Vocal	Visual	Dramatic	Lived Truth (Concretion)	Liturgical Synthesis
Architecture	Bible	Sermon interpreting the intentionality of the text in the form of	Bulletins	Theater games	Identifying the points in our personal social history where the intention of the text becomes concrete	Putting it together as Christian worship
Arrangement of furniture	Key text or text for the occasion	essay	Banners	Sensitivity exercises		Profiles (Orders of Worship)
Lighting	Relation to immediate context	poem	Posters	Happenings		Prayers
Hangings		story	Slides	Creative movement	Family	Music
Paraments for the season of the church year	Setting in reference to Old and New Testaments	dialogue	Films	Excerpts from drama	Church	Offertory
Flowers	Historic commentary on these texts: Augustine, Luther, Calvin, Wesley, et al.	Music performed live recorded	Collages	Dance	Government	Concerns of the congregation
			Representational and nonrepresentational symbols		Business	The Sacraments: Baptism The Lord's Supper
	Other commentary				Attitudes and behavior patterns	
					Symbolic culture traits	The Sending Forth into the World
					Utilitarian culture traits	
					Code of oral or written specifications[18]	

Planning for Worship

Day	Biblical Resources	Vocal	Visual	Dramatic	Lived Truth	Putting It Together Liturgical Synthesis
	Texts	Sermon	Master images	Theater games	Surfacing concerns	Outlining the profile or order of worship
	Other commentary	Story	Banners	Sensitivity exercises	Family	
			Posters	Happenings	Church	
		Dialogue	Slides	Dance	Business	
			Films	Other	Government	
		Other	Other		Other	

Note: This chart shows how these elements of liturgical language may come together in planning for worship. See also chapter 8, "Getting It Together," for a practical programmatic arrangement of this material.

sentence down on paper, his whole morning's labor on a single paragraph, and you know that his creativity was paid for at a great price. That price has to be paid by anyone who is serious about words, and those who do not believe it are not likely to be of much help here. Creativity and critical construction go together in any matter of verbal significance.

Those who hold that any critical approach to *religious* language is blasphemous are another likely source of objection. They are convinced that if they open their mouths, God will fill them. Martin Luther once fell prey to this notion and did not prepare his sermon. Later he confessed that God had indeed filled his mouth— with hot air! An answer to such objections is found conclusively in—of all places—the Bible. Few views could be more distorted than the one that holds that the language of the Bible was handed down from heaven word for word and is universally flawless. It is clear to responsible scholars that the Bible is in fact an immense record of linguistic trial and error. "Biblical language," far from being a monolithic structure, expresses the attempts of many persons in many situations to give utterance to the Word of God that came to them. A clear but brief account of the experiments with language that are recorded in the scriptures is found in Walter Bauer's introduction to his lexicon.[19] Here, Bauer meticulously shows the theoretical enterprises carried out by the New Testament figures in their attempt to communicate, such as developing new formations, compounding old words with new, adopting foreign words, use of specialized and/or technical terms, and shifts in grammatical structure. If *Koine* Greek at last became sublime, it was not without these agonizing linguistic adventures in which the first Christians participated and which the New Testament makes manifest. It is reasonable to suppose that we shall not come to any similarly expressive language by a less arduous path.

A major difference in our time is that there is no

equivalent of the *Koine* Greek. Or, to be more precise, the analogy to the *Koine* Greek is to be found not in a vernacular but in the new styles of communication represented by the electronic media. It is possible to overemphasize the importance of these media. Marshall McLuhan has claimed that the "medium is the message." Others have argued that the medium is the medium, period. It is still best to go to McLuhan himself, for his main points, admittedly often obscure, have not been made clear by a great deal of discussion.[20]

I believe that the understanding of reality and language we are advancing here keeps us from being impaled on either the verbal or the visual horn of a dilemma. The verbal and the visual in this understanding are layers or means of expression that are in continuity. Certainly McLuhan is correct in observing the ways in which the media of film and television and radio affect the way in which reality is perceived and communicated.

However, our emphasis upon the visual is prompted not only by an awareness of what such contemporary commentators are observing, but upon the nature of perception itself. Ray Hart in his major work *Unfinished Man and the Imagination*[21] stresses the "focal actuality" by which truth is known. There is a certain specific concrete imagery that touches off our understanding of reality.

It is on this basis, as much as an awareness of the unparalleled opportunity that the contemporary media give us, that we stress the visual as a key in communication. The imagination is the means by which the self images its visual clues. As Hart points out, a master image is not that *which* is known, but rather that *by* which something is known. Images are a form of horizon through and in which things are known. They are "insights" rather than completed bodies of vision. While a good deal of stress will be placed upon visual images and icons in the ensuing discussion it should always be remembered that they are used with this understanding. Imagination is a function. At this point in history our major task is not to finalize the images of faith, but to activate the imagination.

In thus emphasizing the visual, however, we may seem to be at war with the verbal. Rudolph Arnheim, in his monumental study, insists that visual thinking is categorically different from verbal thinking.[22] Arnheim discusses the logic of images. Arnheim insists that audible information is quite limited, giving us no more than the song of the bird. For Arnheim "vision is the primary medium of thought."

This would seem to be directly and irretrievably at odds with those for whom the verbal is the primary medium of thought. Certainly the integrity of visual thinking, as well as the integrity of what we may call verbal thinking, needs to be preserved. However, if our understanding of language is that of word event, as outlined above, then we can see how the verbal and the visual are both related.

We may see this more clearly if we consider the conflict that sometimes develops between those who insist on the primacy of preaching in worship and those who argue that the oral sermon needs to be replaced by film, multi-media, etc. For some there is a great gulf between the two, and some are willing to throw out the sermon completely for film.

Such a view completely misunderstands both preaching and film. It is precisely from those who have mastered the meaning of film that we may come better to understand what language is about. The Film Sense by Sergei Eisenstein is an acknowledged classic. Here Eisenstein outlines his theories, which have become germinal for much of modern film. At the base of Eisenstein's film sense is montage. The property of montage consists in the fact that two film pieces of any kind when placed together combine inevitably into a new concept arising out of that juxtaposition.

The Odessa-steps sequence of Eisenstein's great film *Potemkin* is an oft-cited example of montage. Here we see the film moving back and forth between a baby carriage rolling down the steps and the soldiers with their guns. Anyone who sees that scene is likely never to forget it.

Now where did this genius of the modern film, Eisenstein, gain his original understanding of montage that has so shaped the world of film, television, and the electronic media? Eisenstein's own answer to this question is unequivocal: "Man and the relationships between his *gestures* and the *intonations* of his voice, which arise from the same emotions, are our models in determining audio-visual structures, which grow in an exactly identical way from the governing image."[23]

In the most sophisticated understanding of the audio-visual, then, we discover not the denial of language as it is spoken and gestured, but its most enthusiastic and creative affirmation.

What we are seeking in the liturgical language that we are suggesting here is essentially what Eisenstein called montage. We are seeking for that combination of word, visual image, sound, gesture, social responsibility, etc., which gives rise to a new understanding of the world and our place in it. We are seeking what Kohler and other psychologists have called the Gestalt.[24] That is an insight into reality that gives rise to a pattern of behavior.

The Gestalt is a combination of the elements in a new configuration. What is called for is a "line" on the elements in the language that gives rise to the whole that is our vision of the world. It could never be hoped that all the elements in the whole could be somehow condensed into a few images or cataloged in a precise fashion. We are not seeking some absolute combination of images. We are seeking rather those few elements verbal, visual, visceral, which can combine in such a way that a new vision of the world is born.

5 Values in the Verbal

One major means of expression of the larger understanding of language is to be found in the proclamation of the Word.[1] People are coming to understand that the use of media such as film strips and/or recordings add dimensions to the spoken Word rather than obliterate it. Thus, it is becoming increasingly common to see the spoken Word augmented by a wide range of other means of communication.

There were some who predicted a few years ago that the rise of audio-visual would mean the death of the spoken Word. They felt that films and other electronic media were so varied and exciting that the spoken Word would not have a chance alongside them. Exactly the opposite has happened. The use of electronic and other media in communication has served to dramatize the importance of the spoken Word and has been a fundamental factor in the renewal of preaching. A conflict about whether preaching should be verbal or nonverbal is really artificial. Clifford Elliot, pastor of the Metropolitan United Church of Canada in Toronto, is only one example of a minister who is equally adept at delivering a sermon in the traditional form and helping a congregation develop a drama that might be used in place of a sermon. He believes that there should be no hangup here. There's more than one way to get the job done.

It has been suggested that the distinction should be made between vocal and nonvocal language since all language is verbal. This distinction divides language that is meant to be vocalized from language that is meant to be expressed through movement or some other form. I gather the force of this particular distinction. However, I will use the distinction between verbal and nonverbal language here because I think it protects the important point made by Arnheim and others that visual thinking is of a different order than verbal thinking.

What I am aiming for is a synthesis beyond the verbal and the nonverbal, and in order to achieve that synthesis ultimately the distinction has to be preserved in a way in which the vocal and nonvocal does not.[2] This is a fruitful quest because it opens up possibilities in language that are obscured when we think of words only as descriptions of objects. It is also a necessary quest both because the verbal clarifies the nonverbal (one hopes, without reducing its mystery), and because so much of worship is verbal in character. Much is spoken in worship, and a good deal is written. The question, therefore, is, What are characteristics of verbal language as it functions in proclamations and liturgy generally that best express the values of meaningful worship?

Imaginal

The imaginal word is the verbal image, that which appeals primarily to the imagination. Metaphors, similes, figures of speech, and analogies generally fall into this category. Caroline Spurgeon in a study of Shakespeare defines "image" in a way that helps us understand why it is so useful in preaching.

We know that, roughly speaking, it [the image] is, as I have said, the little word-picture used by a poet or prose writer to illustrate, illuminate and embellish his thought. It is a description of an idea, which by comparison or analogy, stated or understood, with something else, transmits to us through the emotions and associations it arouses, something of the "wholeness," the depth and richness of the way the writer views, conceives or has felt what he is telling us.[3]

Here are two examples of highly imaginal language. The first is a prayer from Wesley Taylor:

L: From slavery to schedules, duties, and deadlines; from the tyranny of the telephone and the rule of wristwatches,

C: From bondage to busyness, to all things that simply must be done before we stop to think, feel, or care,

L: Good Lord, liberate us into real freedom.

C: From the prisons of old patterns—locked-in ways of doing and responding,

L: And from the domination of our moods—the blahs, the tension, the gnawing of worry, discouragement, and from the treadmill and the roller coaster,

C: God, deliver us and create us a new—free and open to new and joy-filled living.[4]

Kathryn Rogers Deering employs richly imaginal language in this following proclamation. As in the preceding prayer, the images gather up many of the aspects of our daily life and bring faith as close to us as the "sunshine on a cold winter's day," and closer even than our wristwatch.

Anyone who has ever really gotten serious about this Christianity business, who has ever stepped out on a few limbs of faith, knows what a problem *doubts* can be. Doubts can saw the limb of faith right off, causing the Christian to come crashing to the ground. They can be compared with many things:

Doubts are the greasy fingerprints on your camera lens.
Doubts are the dirt in your wristwatch which prevents it from keeping good time.
Doubts are the gravy stains on your new white tablecloth.
Doubts are the mold on that piece of bread which has been left too long in your cupboard.

Doubts are the bulletholes in the windshield of your geta-way car.

Doubts are the weeds in your garden—you have to keep pulling them out.

Doubts are the keys of your piano with the ivory knocked off.

Doubts are the bent dimes which clog up your Coke machine.

But troublesome as they may be, doubts ultimately make us *stronger* by challenging us to new heights. And our Lord never lets his children be challenged too far. Doubts can never win when he is on your side in the inner battle.

Praise the Lord![5]

Oral

All words become oral in one sense merely by being spoken, but what is specified here is that word which is *best suited* to oral delivery. Almost everyone recognizes that human beings normally converse in a manner different from that in which they write. Nevertheless, many preachers do not pay enough attention to the differences between literary and oral style. Sermons sometimes sound like the following sentence, which appeared in a book review where it was perfectly at home: "Despite certain proclivities toward 'neomedievalism' (also illustrated by the counterpart Cambridge movement in church architecture), the best among the Tractarians were grappling with problems which have again become topical in the ecumenical movement and the Second Vatican Council: the relation of scripture to tradition, the role of the sacraments in God's saving activity, the historic nature and order of the church vis-à-vis the incarnation, the definition and authority of the church's symbols (i.e., creedal statements) and dogma, and the church's mission in and for the world (exacerbated for the 19th-century Anglicans by the Erastian issue)."

The differences between this passage and the three immediately below is the difference between literary and oral style. Literary style (at least of this technical

sort) can rely on indirect reference, strings of polysyllables, long and complex sentences. Oral style must be
direct, ration polysyllables, and use brief units of speech
for emphasis. In a useful study, Rudolph Flesch has
noted the following characteristics of oral style: use of
contractions (i.e., I'm, you're, here's), loose sentence
structure, a great deal of repetition, sentence fragments,
and run-on sentences.[6]

Such a design is evident in this Call to Worship by
Frank A. Nickel, Jr.

Leader: Let us rejoice!

People: Why should we rejoice?

Leader: We should rejoice because Jesus is living.

People: What difference does that make?

Leader: The difference between life and death. When we turn
to him in faith and confess our sin, we are forgiven.
Recall his words to one such person: "This very day
you will be with me in Paradise." That's the difference, hope in the place of despair.

People: Let us rejoice and sing![7]

The same quality is evident in this Call to Worship
by Frank M. Witman:

Leader: "Behold, I stand at the door and knock. . . ."

People: How was that again?

Leader: "Behold, I stand at the door and knock. . . ."

People: What is that supposed to mean?

Leader: It means that God is always seeking us.

People: And if he is seeking us, and has found us, what then?

Leader: We are the objects of God's search—but we are
persons—not things. We must respond. God does not
force us.

People: The first step, then, is from God, and the response is
our responsibility?

Leader: Right! And this is what worship is about. To open

doors through which the spirit of God may move, and
we can respond.

People: So be it.[8]

Again Kathryn Rogers Deering is helpful in this
passage from a proclamation in which she effectively
uses the vernacular. The extent to which such language
could be used in corporate reading is debatable, but it
seems appropriate as used here and is a striking illustration of oral style.

Guy #1: ... Whaddya mean, you're "saved"? Ya crazy or
somethin'?! You're the *last* person I would'a thought
would be susceptible to this Jesus bug— Now ya
won't have fun any more; now ya gotta waste Sun-
days in church; now ya gotta pray n' stuff; now ya
won't even laugh at my jokes—Ya must be outa your
head—My *God*, man!

Guy #2: (gently, with a smile) "*My* God, man . . . ."[9]

Experimental

The language of worship should be in touch with
the growing edges of language. Language is always in
process, always changing. Yet to an almost incredible
degree preaching has stayed within the linguistic bar-
riers set up before 1900. Vast numbers of sermons are
prepared as if T. S. Eliot had never written *The
Wasteland*, nor James Joyce *Ulysses*, nor Thomas Pyn-
chon *Gravity's Rainbow*. It is a sure bet that the language
for which we cry is not going to appear unless preachers
crash boldly into *this* side of the twentieth century.

The rapidity with which language shifts will mean
that we shall hardly be able to keep up with all the new
directions—someone in the congregation or the clerical
brotherhood will always be able to be linguistically more
"in" than most of us. But reading the journals devoted to
preaching quickly convinces us that our problem is

hardly that of overuse of contemporary speech. We clearly need to be radically more experimental in our use of language. We need to learn from those who have the ear of the land: the sports writers, the comedians, the pop song writers—especially poets like Bob Dylan. It will help to be in touch with the sub-cultures where the language of tomorrow is being formed, i.e., among the "kids." Such experimentation will likely be shocking to some, and it may also miss before it starts to hit the target. But the *Koine* Greek shocked the elite who thought that Attic was the only proper language. And we have been warned that the language that liberates at last is likely to horrify at first.

Experimental language in worship is language that pushes words beyond their ordinary usage to a depth of meaning. John Killinger is a master of language, experimental and otherwise. This following prayer has much of the playful richness of James Joyce. Words tumble over one another, defying quick surface recognition but beckoning us into the depths.

> Thou Father further fathomed fury
> farther furor felt as substance depth and meaning
> of our common life strife stripped tripped and
> whipped humiliated humbled too death for us and
> life ripe with contumescence of our damaged
> damned and dumbned selves
>   hold hope as help for wholpen eyes and
> solace solstice to our sore distress
>   disdain us not our distant stance
> dance prance from pramble without preamble or
> preemption save salve revolve our valued souls
> and teach reach instill us life at the center at
> the re-radial point where existence becomes
> eternity without dimension of breadth or length
> but deep deep deep plunging lunging into depths
> primordial and without time
>   where thou alone art God and all in all world
> without world and end without end not now but
> forever amen.[10]

The following prayer, by Susan Staff, is experimental in its subject matter, as well as its choice of words. That is, she pushes us beyond the boundaries of politeness, in which prayer is so often imprisoned, to deal with everyday realities. Moreover, there is the irony of her play on Rudyard Kipling's "Recessional."

> Lord of welfare and picket line
> of corporate business large and small
> of factory waste and sewage plant
> of transit strike and pall
> Be thou our guide on littered streets
> jostled by nameless masses
> lest we forget our brother's face
> and shun him when he passes.
> Lord of rapist and general
> of president and whore
> of hustler, pimp, and socialite
> of junkie rich or poor
> Thou art the Savior of us all
> the plastic and the true
> Lest we forget lest we forget
> what love unleashed can do.[11]

Simple, Balanced by the Values of Complexity

The simple word is the one that gets right to the point. Professor Lambuth of Dartmouth advised his students, "If you have a nail to hit, hit it on the head." This goal of simple speech is shared not only by preachers but also by tax collectors. The United States Revenue Service had difficulty with those assigned to communicate with persons about their taxes. Professor Calvin D. Linton was called in to set down some rules for them, and his advice was summed up in two words, "Write simply."

Dr. Linton told the authors to avoid words "which have wrapped robes and trains about their muscular little bodies," like "motivational" for "motive." Henry David Thoreau's motto, "Simplify, simplify, simplify," holds true for all who want to communicate.

However, the communicator must also be sensitive

to the positive values of complexity. Merriam-Webster's *Seventh New Collegiate Dictionary* states that the word *complex* "suggests the unavoidable result of a necessary combining or folding and does not imply a fault or failure."

No preacher who takes theology seriously will be able to avoid the complex. Good theology is simply not all simple. Any real teaching ministry will demand the use of complex words, complex sentences, and complex ideas. The reason we have "big words" is that they say most precisely what we mean. Reconciliation, for example, is a one-word summary of God's enormous deed in Christ. But reconciliation is not a simple word or a simple process. The preacher's task is not to avoid such words but to interpret them so that they truly teach. The language of worship should aim at simplicity, but it should act responsibly toward the complexities of the reality it seeks to express. Anyone who tries to speak "simply" without at the same time being aware of the positive values of complexity will soon discover that "simple" may mean not only "plain" but "foolish."

The simple and the complex are also present in an Affirmation of Faith from James Evans McReynolds. This Affirmation of Faith is a responsive reading, or perhaps more accurately an antiphonal one. The movement from side to side by the congregation dramatizes the complex movement behind such simple affirmations as "God is alive."

(Start in a whisper, right answering left. Get louder at each phrase until we are shouting in the end.)

Left	**Right**
God is alive.	His spirit is afoot.
Life is alive.	Salvation is here.
Hope is alive.	A new age is dawning.
Love is alive.	Death cannot harm us.
We are alive.	New life is given.
God is alive.	New birth is afoot.
Church is alive.	God stirs within it.

Values in the Verbal

Joy is alive.
Church is alive.
God is alive.
Hope is alive.
Life is alive.
Church is alive.

Redemption is here.
Fire within it burns.
We love without masks.
Love is alive.
We are alive.
God is alive.[12]

Clear, Balanced by the Values of Ambiguity

Clear language is free from verbal encumbrances. *Clarity* has probably been the highest linguistic virtue among teachers of homiletics. Halford Luccock once noted as inspired the typographical error that rendered the phrase from I Corinthians 13, "Though I speak with the tongues of men and of angels, and have not *clarity*, I am become as sounding brass, or a tinkling cymbal."[13] It is not hard to see why: clear language is easily understood, and the sermon aims at understanding. The clear word is *the* word for the subject being discussed—the right word. As Mark Twain remarked, the difference between the right word and the almost right word is the difference between the lightning and the lightning bug.

However, as the title of a recent volume by linguistic analysts proclaims, "clarity is not enough."[14] Clarity is not enough, because that which we are seeking to be clear about must itself come under scrutiny. Scrutiny may disclose that what we are seeking to be clear about is not quickly given to clarity: reality may be dark, obscure, hidden. This does not deny the virtue of clarity but simply sets alongside it the value of ambiguity, to which the preacher must also be sensitive. Let me be clear about this: I am not endorsing foggy thinking and hazy speech, which results from laziness and sloppy habits of thought. There is already too much of that, and it has to go. To speak of the positive value of ambiguity is to recognize the inherent mystery within reality, which always seeps through the walls of precision. The intentional ambiguity of which the poets speak is a rhetorical means of coming to grips with the fundamental mystery of being. It requires more thought and discipline on the part of the speaker if it is to be effective. In a famous study, William Empson identifies seven types of ambiguity.[15] This work is a useful corrective to those who praise only clarity, as it analyzes how ambiguity has been used by Chaucer, Shakespeare, Milton, Johnson, Keats, Yeats, Hopkins, Eliot, and others of a noble company.

Another source for the study of intentional ambiguity is the Bible. The riddles of the Old Testament, the apothegms of "The Preacher," the poetic flights of the Psalmist, the often enigmatic utterances of Jesus, the double entendre of John's Gospel, the symbolic action of the Revelation—all these are rhetorical modes of drawing the hearer into the act of perception, touching his sources of motivation, and directing him toward a reality that does not lie easily on the surface of thought.

In worship we should try not so much to get rid of ambiguity as to order it. We should submerge ourselves to the depth of the text and ascend through successive stages toward illumination. And, as Empson observes, the need for clarity is strengthened when seen alongside the values of ambiguity.

The following Call to Worship is clear. Yet, in such phrases as "Let us Celebrate the Unknown" there is intentional ambiguity.

Leader: Let us gather in the memory that we are called to be the people of God.

People: To participate in his mission in the world.

Leader: Let us gather to receive again the lives which are given back to us.

People: That we might be the men and women God intended.

Leader: Let us celebrate the unknown, meeting it with confidence.

People: All this we do because Jesus Christ is Lord![16]

Values in the Verbal

This prayer by Susan Staff is also clear but ambiguous. The imagery is specific, and yet one is left pondering such questions as: Who are the "midnight pretenders"? And where am I in "that wilderness of strangers"?

God, don't let winter into New York City
before the Bowery wino finds a place to sleep
and the Salvation Army can replace his coat,
or landlords turn the heat on in Harlem tenements,
stretch daylight into evening to save the Beekman ambulance
      boys from junkie's knives
guard Madame Park Avenue and Fifi's evening stroll
      by Central Park
and Sister Alexandra walking home through Chinatown,
police the cops who hold down 42nd Street
have mercy on midnight pretenders
and hustlers begging quarters for a drink
this night in all that wilderness of strangers
may someone feel a little less alone.[17]

Concrete

Concrete language speaks to a specific situation and has commitment in view. The language we seek is that which brings not only discernment, but commitment, as Ian Ramsey puts it. Such language not only discloses that there is a man trapped on the ledge below me but that that man is my brother and I must risk my life to save him. This commitment must express itself in our situation, our specific scene in life; and our eyes must be open to the obligations under which we live and the opportunities that are realistically before us. We must be aware of the full range of concretions in our world. Where commitment is not called for in concrete terms that address men and women in the particularity of their existence, nothing happens. Such dislocated language will be heard as were the patriotic speeches to the men in the trenches of World War I, as only "Words, words! They had lost their roots, they no longer culminated in action. And their inefficiency exposed them."[18]

God's Party

The language of worship should be located in the environment of the worshipers and should give rise to responsible action. Observe the prophetic quality in the concrete language used in the following Prayer:

Minister: As men and women who have become phony again since last we gathered, I call upon us all to acknowledge our rejection of the Lord of our lives, to confess our repudiation of the concrete circumstances he has given us, to admit our refusal to be the selves we are. Let us pray.

People: O Lord, our God, we confess that we do not like the bodies we have, we have longed for different families. We would exchange our jobs for others. We would like to do away with parts of our history. We are afraid of our moods and feelings. We wish we had more time. We would like to start over again. We lust after the prestige of others. We think more money will solve our problems. We resent the injustices we have suffered and cherish our sorrows. We want to be appreciated for our small graces. We are enchanted by the past and enticed by the future. We have never really been understood. In short, we have refused to live because we have held out for better terms. Heal us, O God, from the distance we have tried to put between ourselves and life. Restore to us the love of thee and all thy creation. Enable us by thy power to be renewed in our whole lives, through Jesus Christ our Lord. Amen.[19]

The language of worship should be as specific as the language of the daily newspaper. In fact, it may often draw from this source as does this following Prayer of Confession:

Leader: Let us confess in the words of our daily newspaper, the life which is ours and that of our fellowman.

Let us pray:
"Fear of computers nets Internal Revenue six million dollars."

People: O Lord, forgive us our failure to be honest except when there is the danger of being caught.

Values in the Verbal

Leader: "Bodies of two frozen boys found in state."

People: Let us not forget the limitations of our bodies and minds.

Leader: "President urges income tax boost to pay war, domestic plans."

People: We raise up to thee our warped sense of values and our inability to find new patterns for peace.

Leader: "Anti-Mao Reds seize Nanking."

People: We acknowledge that human pain and death within our enemies' ranks do not displease us.

Leader: "Las Vegas blast kills six: officials blame suicide."

People: Keep us mindful that none are immune from ultimate despair nor free from the possibility of injuring another.

Leader: "Mislabeled drug kills twenty patients."

People: In the midst of our pride in technology we confess the imperfections of our systems.

Leader: "Religions sometimes do confuse the issues."

People: We remember that great verbal declarations often fail to become living deeds.

Help us, O Lord, to be conscious and honest about our inadequacies and our natural limitations as well as our deliberate perversions of your will. May we hear the Word that gives us life in the midst of death. Amen.[20]

Discussion of the concrete is a useful transition to our discussion of the larger uses of language because lived truth is the goal of the new liturgical language, whether nonverbal or verbal. We are after what the New Testament calls *doing* the truth. Living the truth is the same as truly living. It is living that life to which liturgy is the clue, a life in which we recognize ourselves as loved by God, confront our brother in his need, and celebrate who God is and what he is doing in our world.

Bernard Berenson knew the Italian painters of the Renaissance as few men ever have. He developed a science of separating the authentic from the inauthentic painters of their period. But Berenson insisted that the purpose of art was not to identify distinguished characteristics on canvas, but to enlarge life. Berenson spoke of "life-enhancement." Art has fulfilled its purpose when it helps plunge someone into a new state of being in which he is more hopeful, more zestful, more radiant, and more intense, not only physically but spiritually and morally as well.[21]

The fundamental problem for worship, we have claimed, is that the reality of worship and the reality of daily life do not come together. Language is the means by which this coming together can take place to give rise to a new history. To bring about this coming together, however, we must have a comprehensive view not only of reality and of language but of who we are as human beings. We turn to men of imagination for help partly because they have sensed our problem in advance of its becoming cataclysmic. Archibald MacLeish, the poet, lamented years ago the divorce between knowing and feeling. Reporters gave us facts, but they did not make us feel them.

"We do not feel our knowledge," he said. "Nothing could better illustrate the flaw at the heart of our civilization. . . . Knowledge without feeling is not knowledge and can lead only to public irresponsibility and indifference, and conceivably to ruin. . . . When the fact is dissociated from the feel of the fact in the minds of an entire people—in the common mind of a civilization—that people, that civilization, is in danger."

Robert Penn Warren emphasized this when he accepted the 1970 National Medal for Literature. Warren commented, "We are bombarded all day long by abstractions, by the truths of advertising men, the politician, the preacher and suddenly we are reminded that every truth that is not lived into, not earned of an experience, either literally or imaginatively, is a lie."

The poet Arthur Gregor puts it succinctly when he

says that what is truth to us is what we know with all of what we are.[22]

In our stress then upon the visual, visceral, and verbal as we seek the image and the gesture, we must never become anesthetized by aesthetics. We must never get lost in the image for its own sake or in the word for its own pleasure. The image, the sensitivity game, the carefully chosen word, are ways of living into the truth.

Too much talk about Christianity has been a truth that has not been known with all that we are. In the living language of liturgy of which we are speaking, breakdown in communication comes not with bad grammar but with a lack of the worshiper's accepting the responsibility for the world and doing so with a sense of eternal support and everlasting joy.

A certain beggar of Paris had his tongue broken during the war and since then lived a subterranean existence under the bridges of the Seine. He came upon a little girl of the underworld who had never heard the story of Christ, and he felt compelled to introduce her to him. When she wandered into a church the beggar placed the little girl before a statue of the Madonna. His face beamed. But the girl's was blank. Startled, the man led the child to a manger scene in one of the chapels. To the little girl, it was just a scene from life she had never known. In desperation, the beggar looked around him. His eyes fastened on the crucifix on the high altar and taking the girl's hand he pulled her toward it. He pointed to the cross. Couldn't the girl see what it was all about? She could not. The meaning was still hidden from her. In deep despair the beggar moaned and began to weep. The greatest story in the world, and he couldn't tell it to a little girl. Then in a terrible fury at himself and the fate that had torn his tongue, he began to beat his hands against his face, clubbing his mouth. Suddenly, the girl cried, "Gigot, stop!" Now both tears and light were in her eyes. She had glanced from the Madonna to the manger to that man upon the cross and the beggar beating his face, and it had dawned on her, the connection between this child who was born in a stable and had grown up to die for others, who could fill men with a fury to share him with others. In the very passion to communicate, the beggar had communicated.

He had managed to combine the visual, the visceral, the gestural into a line that led the girl's gaze to the Christ and to a new awareness of herself. The story suggests how in a time of broken tongues, men with broken tongues may yet lead others into the presence of Christ in a way that enriches life.[23]

6 Worship in
Joy and Sorrow

Weddings, baptisms, and funerals deserve special attention because they represent worship at important points of transition that may be directed to persons who are not regularly "in church."

Two popular children's games of Jesus' day were Marriage and Funeral. Marriage was played with the accompaniment of pipes or flutes. Funeral was accompanied by a good deal of weeping and wailing. But Jesus observed that the children in the marketplace were really only playing with their emotions. He said that his generation was like that. They could neither laugh nor cry with enthusiasm (Matthew 11:16:19).

Modern men and women may be helped to recover the sources of genuine emotion when weddings, baptisms, and funerals are seen as occasions for Christian worship. A good deal of liturgical development today emphasizes this point.

Weddings

New styles of wedding services have been very much in the news. The ones that seem to have gotten the most attention are those which are the most unusual. The charge has been made that some of these new ser-

vices are downright pagan. While this may be true of
some, it seems on the whole that many of the new services for the celebration of marriage represent quite
thoroughgoing study and are the result of genuine
analysis and dialogue.

The wedding of David and Natalie Joranson, for
which Pastor Ken Gelhaus was the celebrant, occurred as
a genuine celebration of marriage.[1] The bride and
groom, best man and matron of honor, and the pastor
assembled in the doorway to greet persons informally as
they arrived, beginning about one half-hour before the
announced time of celebration. A helium-filled balloon
was given each child and a long-stemmed daisy was
given to each adult participant.

At the beginning of the celebration the Communion
table was bare. Helium-filled balloons rose from the end
of the Communion rail, and banners decorated the walls
of the sanctuary. One banner was especially made for the
occasion by the bride's sister.

About the announced time for the celebration, those
distributing flowers took the two remaining bouquets to
the front where they were placed upon the Communion
rail. Friends of the bride and groom took two of their
favorite candles and placed them on the Communion
table.

The pastor stepped forward and took his place behind the table facing the congregation. He carried a
"marriage candle," which was his gift to the bride and
groom. Then the bride and groom came forward, and
each lit his own individual candle. They personally welcomed the congregation and then introduced the pastor
to the congregation. The pastor gave words of greeting
and celebration. The bride and groom then exchanged
rings, without pastoral assistance. Each expressed in his
own way his personal commitment to their marriage
relationship. The pastor then expressed his affirmation
of their marriage relationship on behalf of the faith, the
community, and himself. Together the bride and groom

lit the marriage candle, each using his own candle.

The pastor invited others in the congregation to reaffirm their commitments in love in whichever of three modes would be most meaningful: (1) speaking privately to one another as they remained in the pews; (2) standing where they are, expressing themselves verbally and/or nonverbally; (3) coming forward to join the bride and groom around the Communion table and expressing themselves in commitment to each other. The best man had brought a host of small candles, unannounced to anyone beforehand, including the bride, groom, and pastor, so that couples who had come forward were able to use the same symbol as that of the bride and groom. About half of the congregation came and shared around the table.

The invitation was then given to all present to join the bridal party in the adjacent room, where the certificates would be signed. Each person present was invited to "witness" the marriage by placing his signature on a long scroll paper. The celebration moved downtown and continued with the reception at a local restaurant.

Music was furnished by a guitarist who wandered informally across the rear of the sanctuary as guests were arriving, playing "Wedding Song." He also played as the bride and groom came forward at the beginning, and played and sang quietly but joyfully during the signing ceremony.

Those who were present experienced the mood, which was primarily one of honesty. Nothing was faked or contrived. It was all deeply personal. This wedding ceremony was a richly honest experience of joy in the Lord and in one another. The pastor and the bride and groom who prepared the service did offer this warning to anybody who might attempt something similar: it takes hours of effort and thought. But it's well worth it!

Don Collins, of the United Ministry in Higher Education at Wisconsin State University in Oshkosh, has participated in a number of the new services and offers further advice. These services tend to reflect the openness and contemporaneity of the students with whom he works. As the wedding service is developed in the interaction between the students and the minister, Collins emphasizes four points:

1. The celebration of marriage should be set in the context of meaningful liturgy.
2. The celebration should offer the congregation an important place in the total act of worship.
3. The service should recognize the responsibility of the parents and friends.
4. The language should be contemporary.[2]

The service then is expanded to include solos or other music, contemporary readings or acts of celebration.

Baptisms

Baptism is the event in which one comes to life in the family of God.[3] Baptism is the sacrament by means of which the grace of God makes us partakers of his righteousness and inheritors of everlasting life. It is through the event—the word, the water, the pastoral acts, the personal encounters, the faith of the congregation, and the continuing commitment of the participants—rather than in some substance that God's grace is active in baptism. Our Lord expressly pointed out the place of infants in the family of God when he said, "Let the children come to me, and do not hinder them; for to such belongs the kingdom of heaven" (Matthew 19:14 RSV). Baptism is not for infants only, however. Adults who receive this sacrament are also taken into the life of Christ's holy church.

Recently the ecumenical discussions of baptism have become increasingly important. There were those who felt that baptism might be the controversial rock against which the ecumenical ship would shatter. On the contrary, baptism emerged from the discussions of the World Council of Churches as one of the central rallying points of Christian unity. Moreover, the Second Vatican Council reaffirmed baptism as a "sacramental bond of unity linking all who have been reborn by means of it." Thus the phrase "one Lord, one faith, one baptism" is both one of the oldest and one of the most recent affirmations of the central importance of baptism to the life of the church.

Baptism tells us not only about God and about man, but also about the church where God and man meet. When the child is baptized, he becomes a member of the church of Jesus Christ. Methodism uses the term "preparatory member." *Confirmation* is the service in which persons who have been baptized confirm the vows that were made in baptism and commit themselves to accept their responsibilities in the household of faith. Confirmation classes are held to help prepare persons for these new responsibilities. Almost invariably the pastor learns a great deal from the young people as well. One girl summed up her training in such a class with the poignant words, "I have found what I have always been looking for, and his name is God." Confirmation is a sign of our finding the God who has found us in baptism.

Much of the same kind of search and development that has gone on with the sacrament of the Lord's Supper is occurring with the sacrament of baptism. There are changes in word choice, structure, and style. There is sure to be more development in the area of baptism and confirmation as this is one of the areas under greatest discussion now within the denominations and ecumenically. The role of baptism and confirmation in a society where other means of initiation and "rites of passage" are more common is likely to yield a great deal of redevelopment of the service of baptism.

One discussion of baptism that is especially helpful in bridging biblical and contemporary understandings of initiation is by David G. Owen. Owen deals with baptism as symbolic journey, a means of grace, and infant baptism as a responsible tactic. He writes, "Baptism is a means of grace because it is the symbolic vehicle through which I enter the self-conscious people of God, there to be immersed in the Word of Jesus Christ, the style of Jesus Christ, and the community that believes in him."[4]

"An Order for the Celebration of Holy Baptism" prepared for the Consultation on Church Union is especially worthy of study and experimental use.[5]

Funerals

Just as celebrative services of marriage are helping people to learn to rejoice again, so thoughtful funerals or services of memory are helping people learn what it means to mourn in a genuine and therapeutic way.

For example, the service held to honor the memory of the Rev. Edwin H. Witman in Santa Monica, California, clearly followed an order of worship.[6] There was a prelude, and then the procession with the closed, plain, and unadorned casket followed by the eight pallbearers, who included four sons, two granddaughters, one grandson, and a nephew. The call to worship was followed by a hymn, "O For a Thousand Tongues to Sing." There was an invocation and an Old Testament lesson, which was Psalm 100 read responsively. The Affirmation of Faith was selected from Romans 8 and was followed by the Gloria Patri. Second Timothy 4:1-8 was read, as was I Corinthians 13, and then the hymn "Amazing Grace" was sung. A biographical statement was read by a friend of the minister and then a personal word by another friend followed. The anthem was the Hallelujah Chorus from Handel's *Messiah*. There were closing prayers, a hymn, a benediction, and a postlude, which was described as "powerful, exultant music." So it must have been. The service was designed in consultation with others by the Rev. Frank M. Witman, son of the man who was being remembered.

Worship in Joy and Sorrow

There is all the difference in the world between a funeral service that is merely perfunctory and one that is genuine worship. Persons who have lost a member of the family actually have much more freedom to develop the service of the funeral as worship with their pastor than they realize. Often in the event of death itself the simplest thing is done. Actually most funeral directors are open to cooperate with the directions of the family. Perhaps it is especially helpful at this point for the pastor to take compassionate initiative.

As to the funeral service itself, the Worship Commission of the Minnesota Annual Conference suggests the following guidelines:

1. This worship service is a time for facing reality. Death is a disturbing reality. Our faith enables us to meet the challenge of accepting life as it is. Viewing the body at the funeral home and the presence of the closed casket at the service are quiet evidence of death and of man's willingness to stand in the presence of death without fear. However, when the body is not present, a memorial service should be provided.

2. The service should recognize that powerful emotions are at work and it should try to deal with these feelings honestly. Grief is an honorable emotion, common to all people. It is the expression of the feelings we have about the value of life. It recognizes the relationships that are now broken in loneliness. The service should provide the means for a healthy expression of these feelings.

3. The funeral gives Christians an opportunity to express their emotional and spiritual support. In addition to their liturgical value, congregational singing, saying the creed, the use of unison prayers and responsive readings are supportive to the bereaved.

4. The service can be personal without using either a eulogy or obituary.
5. The funeral service should be a time of great affirmation. It should recognize the personhood of the deceased. Our faith declares that this is not a time of defeat or despair. Here is an opportunity to declare in the most positive way the faith that undergirds and gives meaning to all of life. Careful selection of scripture can relate present suffering to sources of strength. The hymnals have a few hymns listed for funerals. There are many good hymns which might be sung by either the congregation or a soloist. The total service should encourage people to stand in the presence of death with faith and courage.[7]

The 1964 *Methodist Book of Worship* has an Order for the Burial of the Dead. It reflects many of the requirements listed above. A more contemporary order to worship that might be adopted or expanded upon is found in *Ventures 2.*

The church sanctuary is the most fitting and proper place for the final service of one of its members. The place of worship, baptism, confirmation, marriage, and communion is the appropriate place to commemorate the closing of physical life. The sanctuary itself offers a supportive and strengthening influence to the bereaved, and the church reminds us that God embraces us in all the joys and sorrows of life.

Funeral Arrangements. There is increasing use of a funeral pall. The pall serves two purposes. It covers the casket with the symbol of Christ in the same way that a soldier's casket is covered with the flag of his country. It removes the show of importance from the casket and thereby serves as a visible symbol that "God has no favorites."

Churches are also increasingly encouraging the use of memorials in place of the elaborate use of flowers.

Church memorial committees can provide a list of appropriate memorials to which a person might contribute. Flowers are a symbol of the Resurrection and thus are appropriate. Many churches now limit the use of flowers in the sanctuary to those provided by the family as an added expression of their faith. Any additional flowers are left in the vestible.

Because the service is complete as ordered, services of fraternal organizations should be conducted apart from and prior to the services of the church. The local church commission should establish a policy regarding this.

7 How Do We Get to the Party?
The Process of Change

Desire for more meaningful worship is evident all around us. But how do we get to God's Party from where we now are? Practically speaking, perhaps the greatest obstacle to meaningful worship is the understanding of tradition and change that is operative in many congregations. Statements such as "But we have always done it this way" or "I don't think so and so would like it" or "This was a memorial gift in honor of a beloved man" may actually tend to block meaningful worship as much as faulty understandings of language and reality.

If we want more meaningful worship, then, we must pay attention to the process of change—the means by which we get from where we are to where we ought to be in our worship. Where attention is not paid to this matter, fruitless controversy may develop that can actually set back the worship and the entire church program. There are some ways of trying to create change that are self-defeating and tend to call forth reaction.

For example, if changes are made arbitrarily by the pastor or by some other individual without sensitivity to the corporate character of the congregation, the results may be devastating. I heard of a young pastor who was convinced, on the basis of his theological studies, that the chancel of the church he was serving should be divided. The laity tended to oppose this, preferring to retain the communion rail which semicircled around the pulpit and communion table. One Sunday morning the young pastor simply showed up with a saw and divided the chancel—literally. He also divided the church. He was successful in bringing about a change in the architecture that, abstractly considered, may have been more theologically acute. But he failed to see the more important elements of human responsibility and pastoral leadership. Nor are pastors alone in such attitudes. Individual laymen or groups who simply insist on keeping things the way "they have always been" present the same hazard to meaningful worship.

The real point of the liturgical revolution currently underway is that liturgy is coming to be regarded, more radically than ever, as the work of the people. That is, we are now saying that liturgy is the work of the people, not only in that laymen participate widely in the service, but in that they actually share in its shaping, execution, and implementation in the world. The worship of the church needs to reflect this broad participation of the congregation, then, in the preparation of the liturgy as well as in the execution of it.

After considerable reflection upon this matter I have reached the conclusion that the process of change in worship may be more important than the product of change. That is, the process by which a congregation and its professional ministry wrestle through the meaning of their worship may be more important than a particular service of worship that evolves. There may be, in small churches at large across the land, services that are conservative or even reactionary in contrast to what the avant garde may be doing in Greenwich Village or San Francisco. They are part of a liturgical revolution, however, if they represent the honest grappling of their congregation to be faithful in its worship to God in the time and place in which he confronts them now.

"New forms of worship," in themselves, ought not

to be the primary concern. A primary concern is with new people and with new churches. The quest for new forms of worship may be part of the renewal of Christians and of the Christian church, but it is persons and their quest for more meaningful faith, rather than forms of worship in themselves, that are at the center.

The Creative Process

How do we go about creating new forms of worship? One has to answer this question with an immediate additional question—How do we go about creating new forms of anything? The creative process is a great mystery, and those who seem to create best often know least about it. This is not an attempt to be evasive to persons who want a very technical answer. It is simply honest recognition of the truth. No really worthwhile forms of worship are going to be created mechanically. There will be pain and suffering en route to creativity.

Joyce Carol Oates, one of the most prolific writers of our time, states: "The process of creating art cannot be understood, cannot be explained in rational or scientific terms." However, she goes on to talk about her own creative process in a way that is helpful to us as we think about the creative process of worship. She is convinced, as I am, that there is a tremendous poetry locked up in most people. But how do we get it out, and how do we get it into worship? This creator looks for what she calls the "unique universal." That is something that is unique in her own experience that yet somehow strikes a universal depth. She begins with something that is real in her experience in a definite place and time. Her novel *Wonderland*, for example, began with a newspaper item she read. Then she "dreams" about the event, fantasizes about it. There is what she calls a "strange, uncanny, intuitive stage" of just letting the event work through her. Then she does a first draft out of an "original, spontaneous desire." The second writing, and then the third, are more "intellectual, more concerned with the organizing of the materials so that it may communicate to others."[1]

Everyone who creates material for worship, whether it be a call to worship or a sermon, goes through some process of finding that event or experience or scripture that captures the imagination. Then there's a time of letting it play through the mind and the subconscious, an attempt to verbalize, to test in relationship to other people, and finally to put into a shape in which the personally unique may merge with the universal response in people.

The creative process in worship, as we shall see, is distinguished from creative writing like a novel not so much in the dynamics of creativity as in the fact that creation of material for worship tends to occur within a group. To be sure, an individual creates, but by and large the context for the creation of new material tends to be the group.

To show just how individual and group creativity merge in planning for worship, I would like to quote at length from a letter from Carol Goodwin, of Charlottesville, Virginia, who helped lead Wesley Church into some very creative paths in worship.[2]

I wanted to take this opportunity to share a few thoughts with you concerning experimental worship now that I've had a few months off the official job of work area chairman. (We have a new baby at home, and time and energy for things other than family responsibility is a rare bird.) I want to pass these things from my experience on to you before diapers and nursery rhymes crowd them out.

It is so important to have the congregational involvement in the planning, but it is much effort for the leaders. It is much easier to "do it yourself" (also hang-ups on who gets the credit—Heaven help our vanity) than to consciously and deliberately encourage the ideas and thoughts of others who may be less confident about their ability. This selection from Lao Tzu's *Tao Te Ching* says what I mean:

"The best of all rulers is but a shadowy presence to his subjects.

Next comes the ruler they love and praise:
Next comes the one they fear;
Next comes one with whom they take liberties
When there is not enough faith, there is lack of good faith.
Hesitant, he does not utter words lightly,
When his task is accomplished and his work done
The people all say, 'It happened to us naturally.' "

Good psychology from 6th century B.C. No vanity problem
either. The attitude of the minister, work area chairman, other
"rulers" can make a beautiful difference. Their attitude and
then, very basically deeper than the surface, the right climate
needs to be cultivated before creative work will happen and for
the person in the congregation to be motivated.

The creative process must be a fantastic area to learn
about! There are two nonverbal types of attitudes or feelings
that seem to make a big difference. For one, trust. Just making
trust. People, even children, can feel when it is "safe" to reveal
yourself honestly. And ideas about one's "ultimate concern"
are not usually the first thing people share. There is a risk in
giving yourself, be it an idea to a service of worship (a litany or
poem from one's level of experience and understanding) or
one's time and energy to a cause. It may be misunderstood,
rejected, ridiculed. With trust there, egos won't be shattered if
an expression of worship is not appreciated or is inappropriate.
If trust is operating among the people of the worshiping community, personal inadequacies won't matter so much, and
change and growth are less painful, too.

The other thing that seems so basic to the creative revelation is a sense of possibility. We can be encouraging about
ourselves and each other and our effect on the institution. If we
can believe that we can make a difference, that the answer is
not to abandon the old structures when they seem so
hopelessly inappropriate to our lives, but to patiently discover,
explore, finding a sense of community in the process. Your
effort with *Ventures* is a flower blooming in a crumbling,
rundown building. The problem that young people who assume position of responsibility in the local church is we don't
like their being threatened and over-reacting and they don't
like our being impatient. We turn each other off. It turns us
(frustrated) away from the institution and they become even
more closed. The sense of possibility is crushed and the only
thing created is a bunch of ugly, hostile feelings. Many times
instead of finding each other and communing, we lose each
other and any constructive changes in worship. I feel a real
sense of urgency about the need for taking the lifestyle of hope,

love, and justice seriously through the church. Where are the forces of reconciliation going to come from if (when) it crumbles? It is scary when I think about how ineffective the church is in society in general.

Aren't these really "works of art," products of religious or spiritual creativity? To create the capacity in oneself, then to help each other to develop these attitudes of trust and possibility seems to be an art form in itself—maybe Christianity, really operating in a person's life, is the ultimate art form! There are many small works of trust and love—milestones in spiritual growth, a really meaningful response to God. Does worship lead to this or begin with this?

I am very glad that Mrs. Goodwin passed these thoughts on to me and then to the reader before "diapers and nursery rhymes" crowded them out. Not only does the letter expose the genius of the creative process of worship—it itself is an example to me of creative use of language.

Several elements of the process of change become clear as we look at churches across the country that have been able to make significant steps forward in liturgy while maintaining and even deepening their congregational life.[3] We may discern at least eight steps that seem to be followed again and again in these congregations. The presence of *creative* individuals is necessary at every step.

Steps to More Meaningful Worship

Worship. We begin with worship itself. We begin with who we are and where we are, wherever we may be. More meaningful worship grows out of our history of worship, our personal acts of praise and devotion. It is the ongoing life of worship itself and those who have experienced it, even in frustrating moments, that lies at the base of more meaningful worship.

Study in small groups. In virtually every case when significant progress is made to more meaningful worship there is a small group in the church that made an intensive study of the meaning of worship. This small group may be a work area in worship, or it may be a specially constituted study group. The pastor is normally a part of this group. A workshop may be part of the group's study.

The workshop approach is proving helpful as a step toward revitalizing worship. Workshops may be held at the national, regional, district, or cluster level. However they are especially useful at the local church level, where most liturgy takes place. Here is the schedule of a one-day worship workshop planned by William J. Fleming at the United Parish in Brookline, Massachusetts.

9:00   Registration
      An opportunity to visit the Resource Center (Guild Room) and look over displays and the book table.

9:30   Opening Session
      "What Is Worship, What Constitutes Worship?"
        Dr. Robert Luccock, Professor of Homiletics, Boston University School of Theology.
      "Traditional and New Forms: Is There Room for Both?" A panel discussion
      Harry Scott   Arlene Flowers
      Marsha Sherman   Bill Fleming—*moderator*

10:30 Responding in Small Groups *(We will be using the same small groups for both the response sessions and for the Worship Preparation Workshop later this afternoon.)*

11:00 Worship Guidelines

11:20 Responding in Small Groups

12:15 Lunch

1:00 Interest Groups
      Worship Community—Group Dynamics
      The Use of Music

The Environment of Worship
Worship Themes and Resources (*Including Dance, Drama, Media*)

2:00   Interest Groups
Worship Community—Group Dynamics
The Role of Preaching
The Sacraments

2:45   Regathering

3:00   Worship Preparation Workshop
An opportunity to prepare an outline for a worship service. Some groups may want to implement their service at an upcoming worship service in the Parish.

4:00   Closing Worship

Twenty persons attended, including resource leaders. After the workshop Pastor Fleming evaluated it and made some notes for future reference. More persons should have been involved in the planning. There should have been some activity and "doing" sessions. A simple evaluation sheet for immediate follow-up should have been available, and the timing of the event should have been better. Most communities have access to leadership for such events, and the program can be adapted to the local situation.

Gather data from the congregation and others. In addition to the study of biblical, theological, and cultural basis of worship, there needs to be a sampling of how the membership of the church sees worship.

In gathering data, however, concern should be paid not only to those who do attend worship, but also to those who do not. That is, there should be some way of getting the opinions of those members of the church who do not attend regularly. Furthermore, deliberate effort should be made to identify those groups who are not now in the church but who ought to be there. If, for

117

example, there are a number of young adults in the community, none of whom come to church, there needs to be an effort to find out why. Similarly, if there are many elderly around who do not show up, why not? The concerns of evangelism and outreach need to be incorporated into the fundamental planning for worship.

An extensive survey on worship was developed in the Wesley Memorial United Methodist Church in Charlottesville, Virginia. This survey gathers information about personal attitudes, expectations, preferences, and opinions on the elements and the shape of the service. Some gathering of data as to where the congregation is and where they would like to go, is the essential part of the process of change.

Review and create resources. Once the study group has considered the fundamentals of worship and has gathered data from the congregation, attention needs to be given to sources of new material for worship. A listing of resources will be found later in this volume. The *Ventures* series, referred to throughout this study, is especially designed for this purpose.

These volumes are intended basically as guidelines and stimuli for local congregations. It is hoped that, having seen styles by means of which other congregations are going at their task, each specific local group will be able to create materials and thus expand its range of worship. One of the finest things said about *Ventures* came from one who wrote that it gave him "the courage to create."

Creation of new material is especially important at this point. All that has been gathered from others may be a starting point for new journeys. Here individual creativity is called for, as described above by Joyce Carol Oates and Carol Goodwin. Writing assignments may be passed around the group. Even if one person is the "natural" writer in the group, all should make their contributions. The writing itself is best done by an individual, since it is difficult if not impossible to write by committee; but what is written should be reviewed by the committee.

Design the service. Once the resources have been studied and created, new materials and designs should be developed. This is the point at which criteria for meaningful worship should be aimed. Out of the resources that have been gathered and created, which of these seem to be most truly biblical, most historically conscious, most theologically discerning, etc.? (See chapter on criteria.)

1. Among the matters to be decided in terms of exercising the options is the question of whether changes should be introduced at the major Sunday morning service or at an earlier service, or, for that matter, a later one. A service other than the main Sunday Morning service is sometimes used to introduce new materials, but there are certain risks in this. The danger is that a separate congregation may grow up with a liturgical style and interest different from the main group of the congregation. Such may be a necessary step, at least for a time, but eventually, ways of ministering authentically to all the congregations within the congregation need to be developed.

2. What will be the basic arrangement of the service? What profile of order do you plan to use?

3. How will the sanctuary be arranged for the service? Can the pews be moved, and, if so, can they be arranged in a circle or semicircle so as to gain greater intimacy and personal contact with the congregation? Will the service be in the sanctuary, or perhaps in the fellowship room, which might give more freedom of movement?

4. What specific elements of worship will be used within the profile of worship?

5. What media of interpretation will be used to develop the meaning of the text (See the chart Elements of Liturgical Language, p. 78).

6. What music will be used in this service and who will lead us in performance, etc.?

Worship again. The planning needs to be implemented, and the service that has been planned needs to find its expression in the communal worship life of the congregation.

Evaluate. The event of worship must now be tested against the goals and expectations set for it. The group needs to ask itself whether the goals of more meaningful worship, of recognition of oneself, confrontation with one's brother, celebration of what God is doing in the world, or other goals that they have set have been reached and why or why not.

There needs also to be feedback from the congregation as a whole. One way of doing this is by designating feedback groups. In this approach, several persons are asked to serve as part of a feedback group looking for certain elements in the service on which they then report. Of course, a certain amount of feedback will come through oral comment. From time to time, at least, it may be desirable to ask for some kind of written comment from persons who have participated in the service. On the basis of this feedback, then, further plans are made.

Worship! In all our planning and all our creativity, we must never lose sight of the centrality of worship itself. What we are doing arises from worship, and, when it is effective ascends into more meaningful worship. Liturgy may be reshaped in response to the God who meets us in life and calls us to new life. Always the stress is not upon new forms of worship but upon new persons.

Reuel Howe has written, "Cooperation between clergy and laity is a trememdous resource in every aspect of the Church's life, including its worship. The greatest work a church can do is liturgical work, bringing people into a worshiping, responding and renewing relationship to God, man, self, and environment. It is a preview of the Kingdom of God."[4]

How Do We Get to the Party?

Eight Steps to More Meaningful Worship

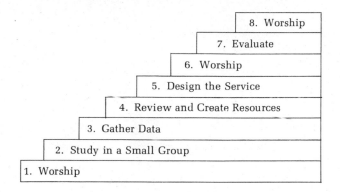

8. Worship

7. Evaluate

6. Worship

5. Design the Service

4. Review and Create Resources

3. Gather Data

2. Study in a Small Group

1. Worship

8 Getting It Together: Options and Resources

Now let us look at the significance of all these concerns by focusing on the group that is meeting to plan for worship. How are they to get together these theological historical, and practical considerations into a meaningful service of contemporary worship?

They will want to consider the options available to them at the key points in the service and exercise the options that most effectively help them fulfill their goals. Let it be said again: exercising the options does not create worship. Worship comes not from a checklist but from God. But worship is work—the work of the people of God, and studies like this can best help us allow God to work within us.

This is a creative process, and every group will vary in its makeup and interest. The following checklist, however, may serve as a practical guide to the matters under discussion in planning more meaningful worship.

Not every area will be dealt with in detail every week. But all are important, and over the course of the year all should be dealt with for the most meaningful worship.

We will begin with some of the fundamental questions with which such a group should wrestle, and proceed to details of planning a particular service.

Getting It Together: Options and Resources

1. What do we understand to be the goals of worship?
   a. Recognition of God's love for us.
   b. Confrontation with the needs of our brothers and sisters.
   c. Celebration of who God is and what he is doing in the world.
   d. Other:

2. What kind of material are we looking for?
   a. Biblically based
   b. Historically conscious
   c. Personally and corporately authentic
   d. Theologically discerning
   e. Missionally sensitive
   f. Liturgically whole
   g. Other:

3. Who are the people for whom we are planning this service?
   a. What are their hopes?
   b. Where are their hurts?
   c. Who is not likely to be there but should be kept in mind?
   d. Are there ways those not often present could be encouraged to come—invitations, transportation, meeting of special needs for those in wheelchairs, etc.

4. What passage or passages of scripture are at the base of this service?
   a. From a lectionary
   b. From a special emphasis in the church's life.
   c. From the pastor's planning
   d. From the group's selection

5. State in a sentence or two the main concern, theme, or idea of this service as you interact with the biblical texts.

6. What music will best serve this concern?
   a. Prelude

   b. Hymns
   c. Anthems
   d. Solos
   e. Postlude
7. What visual aids will best express this theme?
   a. Symbols for bulletin
       Representational
       Nonrepresentational
   b. Banners
   c. Posters
   d. Slides
   e. Films
   f. Collages
   g. Other:
8. What life situation, personal and social, are touched by this theme directly or indirectly?

A

Areas of:
Trust
Fear
Guilt
Work
Leisure
Identity
Despair
Other:

B

Community needs must also be dealt with. What are the basic current issues in such areas as the following.

	Life Situation	Attitudes	Behavior
Family			
Government			
Business			
Church			
Other:			

9. What will be the form of the sermon?
   Solo presentation
   Dialogue *(if so, between whom?)*
   Use as part of or whole sermon:
   Drama
   Film
   Slides
   Sensitivity exercise
   Theater game
   Dance
   Other:

10. What will be our language for
    Call to Worship
    Prayer
    Statement of Faith

11. What actions express our:
    Greeting
    Offering
    Thanks

12. How will we get input from the congregation?
    Sharing of concerns
    Open prayer
    Writing on cards in pews

13. How will basic message relate to personal/social needs?
    Sermon
    Prayer
    Offering
    Hymns
    Concerns

14. How will feedback be gained from congregation?
    Discussion time following same
    Questionnaires
    Cards in pew

15. Will the Lord's Supper be celebrated? If so, according to what order?

16. In what order should the service proceed?

God's Party

(The Test of Liturgical Wholeness)

By identifying the elements of worship in the cluster in which they tend to belong, we can make sense of the order, follow its progression, and better absorb appropriately its meaning. Here are some more possibilities in outline form (details may be found in *Ventures in Worship 2* and 3.).

An Order for Morning Worship

The Church Gathers

> Prelude
> Call to Worship (Introit)
> Hymn
> Invocation
> Call to Confession
> Prayer of Confession
> Personal Confessions—Amen
> Words of Assurance
> The Lord's Prayer—modern version

To Hear the Word of God

> Call to Praise
> Psalter
> Gloria Patri
> Anthem:
> Old Testament Lesson
> New Testament Lesson
> Hymn
> Sermon
> Silent Reflection

To Respond in Faith

> Affirmation of Faith
> Call to Prayer
> Prayer of Thanksgiving
> Prayer of Petition

126

Getting It Together: Options and Resources

Personal Prayers
Collect
Parish Notices
Offering
Doxology
Prayer of Dedication

The Church Scatters

Call to Service
Hymn
Benediction
Postlude

Other Orders

A. 1. The assembling
   2. Our remembering
   3. Receiving
   4. Responding
   5. Covenanting

B. 1. Gathering
   2. Singing Praises
   3. Facing ourselves
   4. Receiving the world as good
   5. Rehearsing the faith of our heritage
   6. A message
   7. Response
   8. Retiring

C. *The Prologue*
   The First Act
   The Second Act
   The Third Act
   The Epilogue
   The Cast
   The Fellowship Time

D. Others:

17. What arrangement of our space allows for the best development of the service?

Congregations that raise this question in the context of planning for new building will find *Architecture for Worship,* by Edward A. Sovik, especially stimulating. Sovik makes a case for a centrum, not a church, a building that provides space that is flexible, functional, and adaptable.

For churches not planning to build, rearrangement of space by movement of pews allows for a great variety of settings which extends the range of worship. Consider these possibilities given in *Sanctuary Planning,* prepared by the Office of Architecture, by Norman G. Byar, then executive secretary. This book was published by The National Division of the Board of Missions of The Methodist Church in 1967, but is still helpful.

At a recent meeting of the former Commission on Worship it was suggested that churches be planned around the following axioms:

UTILITY   A church should be designed for the several types of worship which will be used.

SIMPLICITY Concentrate on the essentials and eliminate the superfluous.

FLEXIBILITY A church should be adaptable for many different services and occasions.

INTIMACY   Our buildings should foster a sense of oneness in the doing of our work.*

The following sketches illustrate ways of accomplishing these means. Apparently maximum use can be made of a rectangular room with a level floor. Not shown in the sketches are such facilities as narthex, sacristy, organ space, choir room,

*Professor James F. White in paper prepared for the Commission on Worship, Dallas, Texas, April 11, 1967.

kitchen or storage areas which would normally be needed. The size and location of these spaces would vary with each architectural solution. To change the character or atmosphere of the room, movable wall panels, light cloth hangings or other devices might be used. The following abbreviations are used:

T=Communion table
P=Pulpit
L=Lectern
F=Baptismal font

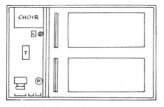

A. FORMAL WORSHIP
All furnishings are portable with the possible exception of the organ console. The emphasis is upon the pulpit, table and font. The nave seats 240 and the choir from 21 to 24.

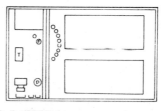

B. BAPTISM
The pastor and the one being baptized would stand on the level of the chancel platform so the ceremony could be seen by the congregation. The parents and sponsors would stand before the font on the nave floor.

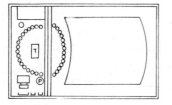

C. COMMUNION
Communion is served by the pastor to the congregation as they stand around the table. The center aisle has been eliminated and the rows of chairs placed 42″ apart allowing 20″ per person.

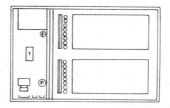

D. COMMUNION
The communicants are served by the pastor at a portable communion rail and kneeling step. The rows of chairs in the nave are spaced 32″ apart allowing 18″ per person.

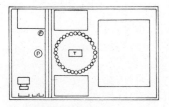

E. COMMUNION
The communion table has been moved down into the nave with the congregation grouped around it. The pulpit has been moved to the center of the chancel platform. Communion could be served standing or the portable rail and kneeling step could be used for kneeling.

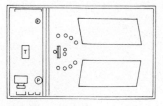

F. WEDDING
The width of the center aisle has been increased from 5' to 7' and the width of the front cross aisle increased to allow adequate space for the bridal party and pastor. A prayer desk or prie-dieu is used for kneeling. This plan seats 98 although the capacity could be increased.

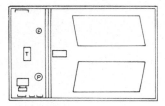

G. FUNERAL
The width of the center aisle has been increased to 7' to allow the pallbearers to bring in the casket. The actual seating capacity would depend upon the need. The normal practice is to place the casket as indicated. perpendicular to the table.

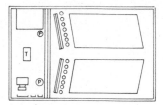

H. RECEPTION OF MEMBERS
Those being received in membership are shown at the communion rail. The same arrangement would serve a confirmation service where kneeling is required.

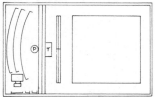

I. EVANGELISTIC MEETING
The congregation has been grouped together in front of the pulpit, which has been placed in the center of the chancel. The choir is grouped in back of the pulpit. The communion table and rail are forward of the pulpit.

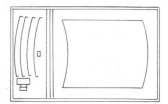

J. CHOIR PROGRAM
The choir is grouped together on the platform facing the choir leader and congregation. Special choir programs (cantatas, oratorios, etc.) are popular in many parts of the country. There is considerable freedom in these plans in providing space for instrumentalists near the choir.

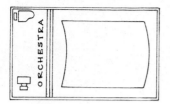

K. CONCERT
Ample space is available in this arrangement for large musical instruments and a piano on the platform.

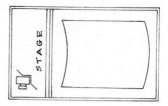

L. DRAMA
The chancel platform serves as a stage for drama, interpretative dancing, church school pageants, etc. In this illustration, the organ console is screened from view.

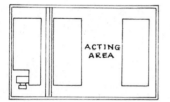

M. DRAMA
The acting area is in the center of the nave and the chancel is used for seating. This is similar to theatre-in-the-round productions.

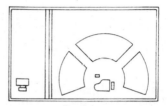

N. GROUP SINGING
For community or groups singing the congregation is grouped around the piano and the song leader.

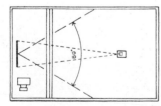

O. AUDIO/VISUAL
The screen is located on the platform so that the majority of the audience would be within the recommended 60° viewing angle. Beyond this angle the picture becomes distorted.

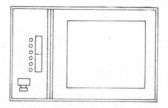

P. MEETINGS
In this illustration two tables have been placed in the center of the platform with the leaders seated behind the tables. This could be used for debates, lectures or church or community meetings.

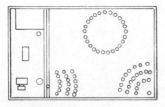

Q. CHURCH SCHOOL
Three classes for youth or adults are shown in different parts of the room. We are assuming that separate classes would be provided for children.

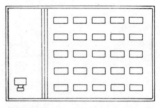

R. STUDY HALL
The 40' x 65' room could also be used after school hours as a study hall. Separate tables are shown for each two to four students, as well as tables for those in charge.

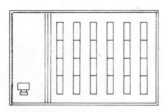

S. DINING
Using standard size tables (30" x 96") the room would accommodate 192 persons allowing 8 persons per table. The 15' x 40' platform could serve for the speaker's table, additional tables or for a program.

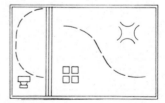

T. DINING
If smaller tables (30" x 72") were arranged with space between each table, the room would accommodate 150 persons allowing 6 persons per table. If the tables were moved together to provide space for 5 additional tables, the room would seat 180 persons.

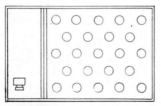

U. DINING
Round tables encourage a greater sense of fellowship since all persons are within conversation range of each other. This arrangement around 48" diameter tables seats 138 at 6 persons per table, or 184 at 8 persons per table.

V. DISPLAYS
The room is arranged for such displays as paintings, sculpture, book exhibits, schools of mission displays, church school exhibits or any other type of exhibition which requires space for large numbers of people and ample viewing areas. The arrangement is planned to encourage the flow of traffic through the exhibitions.

132

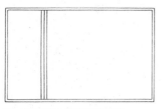

W. GROUP ACTIVITIES
If all the furniture in the rooms were movable, the entire area could be cleared for group activities. This would require ample nearby storage space for all furniture.

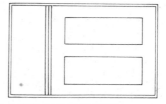

X. MINIMUM SEATING
The use of chairs allows the church to set up seats for the anticipated attendance. For each of these arrangements the room would appear to be full. (12 rows of chairs, 24" per person, 36" per row, seats 144).

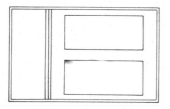

Y. AVERAGE SEATING
By reducing the spacing between chairs and between rows and by reducing the width of aisles, the room would seat 234 persons. (13 rows of chairs, 20" per person, 33" per row, seats 234).

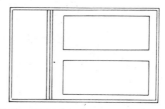

Z. MAXIMUM SEATING
For those occasions requiring maximum seating the chairs are placed closer together. This will still allow ample seating space for most individuals. (15 rows of chairs, 18" per person, 32" per row, seats 300).

18. When shall we meet again to evaluate our worship in the light of our goals and context?

19. Where may resources be found to help us worship and to stimulate our growth?

133

Bibliography

Architecture

Bruggink, Donald J., and Droppers, Carl H. *Christ and Architecture*. Grand Rapids: Eerdmans, 1965

Sovik, Edward A. *Architecture for Worship*. Minneapolis: Augsburg, 1973.

Art Supplies for Liturgies

Christian Art Associates, 1801 West Greenleaf Ave., Chicago, Illinois 60626.

St. Stephen's Church Enterprises, 3805 Warren St., N. W., Washington, D. C. 20016.

Banners and Vestments

Allen, Horace T., Jr. *About Vestments*. Office of Worship and Music, Witherspoon Bldg., Philadelphia, Pennsylvania 19107. 1970.

Anderson, Robert W. and Caemerer, Richard R. *Banners, Banners, Banners*. Christian Art Associates, 1801 West Greenleaf Ave., Chicago, Illinois 60626. 1967.

Ireland, Marion P. *Textile Art in the Church*. Nashville: Abingdon Press, 1971.

Maker of Banners and Vestments

Albert, Martha. 26 Dunlap Road, Park Forest, Illinois 60466.

God's Party

Books

Cox, Harvey. *The Feast of Fools.* Cambridge: Harvard University Press, 1969.

Dix, Dom Gregory. *The Shape of the Liturgy.* London: Dacre Press, 1954.

Hartt, Julian N. *Theology and the Church in the University.* Philadelphia: Westminster Press, 1969.

Hoon, Paul W. *The Integrity of Worship.* Nashville: Abingdon Press, 1968.

Hovda, Robert. *Manual for Celebration.* Luturgical Conference, 1330 Massachusetts Ave., N. W., Washington, D.C. 1970.

Keen, Sam. *Apology for Wonder.* New York: Harper & Row, 1969.

Leonard, George B. *Education and Ecstasy* New York: Delacorte Press, 1968.

Neale, Robert. *In Praise of Play.* New York: Harper & Row, 1969.

Randolph, David J. ed. *Ventures in Worship.* Nashville: Abingdon Press, 1969.

——————., ed. *Ventures in Worship 2.* Nashville: Abingdon Press, 1970.

——————., ed. *Ventures in Worship 3.* Nashville: Abingdon Press, 1973.

Snyder, Ross. *Contemporary Celebration.* Nashville: Abingdon Press, 1971.

Verheul, A. *Introduction to the Liturgy, Towards a Theology of Worship.* Collegeville, Minnesota: Liturgical Press, 1968.

Von Allmen, Jean-Jacques. *Worship: Its Theology and Practice.* New York: Oxford University Press, 1965.

White, James. *New Forms of Worship.* Nashville: Abingdon Press, 1971.

Music

I. Recordings
   New releases are constantly coming out, so this field should be reviewed regularly.
   Abingdon Audio. Graphics, 201 Eighth Avenue South, Nashville, Tennessee 37202
   The Mission Singers
      Disco-Teach. Albums of significant popular songs accompanied by printed leaders guide.
   Avant Garde Records, 250 West 57th, New York, New York 10019

Bibliography

Dust and Ashes
   "The Lives We Share"
John Ylvisaker
   "Cool Livin," secular and spiritual for young
   "Follow Me," songs on New Testament stories
   "A Love Song," scripturally based love songs
Medical Mission Sisters
   "Joy Is Like the Rain," contemporary/religious
   "I Know the Secret," life/sorrow/struggle/joy
Fortress Records, 2900 Queen Lane, Philadelphia, Pennsylvania 19129
   Dick and Don and Singing Friends from Princeton sing songs by Avery and Marsh

II. Hymnals and Songbooks
   Alive and Singing. Richard Avery and Donald Marsh. Port Jervis, New York: Proclamation Productions.
   Contemporary Worship Hymns, I. Inter-Lutheran Commission on Worship for Provisional Use. Minneapolis: Augsburg Publishing House, 1969.
   Discovery in Song. Vol. I New York: Association Press, 1968.
   Dust and Ashes Songbook. Nashville: Abingdon Press, 1971.
   Hymnal for Young Christians, I & II. Chicago: F.E.L. Publications. 1966, 1967, 1968.
   Hymns for Now, A Portfolio for Good, Bad, or Rotten Times. Walther League, 875 North Dearborn St., Chicago, Illinois 60610. 1967.
   Hymns for Now II. Youth Ministry Materials, P.O. Box 14325, St. Louis, Missouri 63178. 1969.
   Hymns for Now III. Youth Ministry Materials, 1972.
   Hymns Hot and Carols Cool. Richard Avery and Donald Marsh. Port Jervis, New York: Proclamation Productions. 1967.
   Mission Singers Song Book. Nashville: Abingdon Press, 1971.
   New Wine, Songs for Celebration. Board of Education of the Southern California-Arizona Conference of The United Methodist Church, 5250 Santa Monica Blvd., Los Angeles, California 90029. 1972.
   Ventures in Song. Ed. David James Randolph with special assistance from Bill Garrett. Nashville: Abingdon Press, 1972.

God's Party

People and Places

Celebration—A Centre of Contemporary Worship, 117 Bloor Street East, Toronto, 285, Ontario, Canada.

Center for Worship Reformation, Wesley Taylor, 1219 Third Street N.W., Salem, Oregon 97304.

The Liturgical Conference, 1330 Massachusetts Avenue, N. W., Washington, D. C. 20005.

The Project on Worship, Box 840, Nashville, Tennessee, 37202.

Periodicals

Celebration. P. O. Box 281, Kansas City, Missouri.

Liturgy. Liturgical Conference, Inc., 1330 Massachusetts Ave., N.W., Washington, D.C. 20005.

Mass Media Bi-Weekly Newsletter. 2116 North Charles St., Baltimore, Maryland 21218, or 1720 Chouteau Ave., St. Louis, Missouri 63103.

Probe. 1880 Arrott Bldg., 401 Wood St., Pittsburgh, Pennsylvania 15222.

Response/in Worship, Music, the Arts. Valparaiso University, Valparaiso, Indiana 46383.

Multi-Media

Babin, Pierre, editor, *The Audio Visual Man* (Dayton, Ohio: Pflaum, 1970).

Bloy, Myron, editor, *Multi Media Worship* (New York: Seabury Press, 1970).

Campbell, Charles, and Huck, Gabe. *Visual and Verbal Meditations.* New Life Films, Box 2008, Kansas City, Kansas 66110.

Moser, Lida, *Fun in Photography* (Garden City, N. Y.: Amphoto, 1974).

Pincus, Edward, *Guide to Filmmaking*, (New York: Signet Books, 1969).

Shamburg, Michael, *Guerilla Television* (New York, Chicago, San Francisco, 1971).

Wells, Robert. *Celebrative Photography: A Family Reunion.*

Notes

1. God's Party

1. Richard L. Sprague, from the Project on Worship.
2. *Ibid.*
3. *Ventures in Worship,* ed. David James Randolph (Nashville: Abingdon Press, 1969); pp. 35-36, from First University United Methodist Church, Minneapolis. (This work will hereafter be referred to as *Ventures.)*
4. *Ventures,* pp. 4-5, from Donald Vroon, Minister, the United Methodist Church, Crosswicks-Ellisdale, N.J.
5. H. Grady Hardin, Joseph D. Quillian, Jr., and James F. White, *The Celebration of the Gospel* (Nashville: Abingdon Press, 1964), pp. 124-25.
6. *Ventures,* pp. 85-90. Cf. Gary W. Barbaree, "The Lord's Supper: A Christian Phenomenon," *Ventures in Worship 3,* ed. David James Randolph (Nashville: Abingdon Press, 1973), pp. 127-41. (This work will hereafter be referred to as *Ventures 3.)*
7. "An Alternate Text for the Lord's Supper or Holy Communion" (Nashville: The United Methodist Publishing House, 1972).
8. In correspondence with the author.
9. (Garden City, N. Y.: Doubleday 1969).
10. See chapter 7 for a summary of learnings on the process of change in worship.

2. Elephants in Church: Goals

1. See Paul W. Hoon, *The Integrity of Worship* (Nashville: Abingdon Press, 1971). Note especially pages 91 to 94 in which Hoon criticizes the concept of worship as "worthship." Professor Hoon's point that worthship may tend to obscure the divine initiative whereby God ascribes worth to man rather than the other way around is well taken. However, granting that, man's awareness of God as being of supreme worth is the fundamental response to

139

God's initiative. It is in this sense that we speak here of worship as the celebration of that which is of worth and Christian worship as the celebration of the gospel of Jesus Christ.

2. *Our Changing Liturgy* (Image Books; Garden City, N. Y.: Doubleday, 1967), p. 17.

3 *Presbyterian Worship: Its Meaning and Method* (Richmond; John Knox Press, 1966), p. 14.

4. Henry C. Horn, "Experimentation and the Congregation" in *Religion in Life*, Spring, 1970, p. 10.

5. *The Meaning of Meaning* (New York: Harcourt, Brace and Company, 1923).

3. Criteria of Meaningful Worship

1. *The Book of Discipline of The United Methodist Church, 1972* (Nashville: The United Methodist Publishing House, 1973), p. 75. This volume shall hereafter be referred to as *The Book of Discipline, 1972.*

In regard to worship the tests of mission and liturgical wholeness have been added. These guidelines seem to be implicit, but are more useful when made explicit.

After the doctrine and doctrinal statements became Part 2 of *The Book of Discipline*, a leader's guide to this material was prepared by the Division of Curriculum Resources. The guide called for the consideration of "New liturgical forms in reflections of living Theology . . ." See *Leader's Guide to Doctrine and Doctrinal Statements*, prepared by John P. Gilbert with Albert C. Outler, Harvey H. Potthoff, and Robert W. Thornburg (Nashville: Graded Press, 1972).

2. The test of Scripture is referred to in *The Book of Discipline, 1972*, pp. 75-76, as follows: "United Methodists share with all other Christians the conviction that Scripture is the primary source and guideline for doctrine. The Bible is the deposit of a unique testimony to God's self-disclosures: in the world's creation, redemption and final fulfillment; in Jesus Christ as the incarnation of God's Word; in the Holy Spirit's constant activity in the dramas of history. It is the primitive source of the memories, images, and hopes by which the Christian community came into existence and that still confirm and nourish its faith and understanding. Christian doctrine has been formed, consciously and unconsciously, from metaphors and themes the origins of which are biblical."

3. See Gerhard Ebeling *Word and Faith* (Philadelphia: Fortress Press, 1963, especially pp. 304-32. See also David J. Randolph, *The Renewal of Preaching*. (Fortress Press, 1969), and an introduction to Gerhard Ebling's sermon Press, 1969), and in introduction to Gerhard Ebeling's sermons on Prayer (Fortress Press, 1966).

4. In his introduction to Elia Kazan, *America, America* (New York: Popular Library, 1964).

5. *Ventures 3*, p. 69.

6. *Ibid.*, pp. 70-72.

Notes

7. Frank Wood's *Litany* based on Psalm 8 is from *Ventures in Worship 2*, ed. David James Randolph (Nashville: Abingdon Press, 1970), p. 88. (This work will hereafter be referred to as *Ventures 2*.)
8. The test of tradition is referred to in *The Book of Discipline, 1972*, pp. 76-77, as follows: "Christian interpretations of the biblical revelation have a complex history. In every age, Christian people have formulated and reformulated their understandings of what they have received in doctrines and liturgies that interact upon each other. All church traditions profess themselves bound to Scripture for their original insights and may rightly be judged by their essential faithfulness to its disclosures. An uncritical acceptance of tradition amounts to traditional-*ism*, deliverance from which requires an adequate understanding of history as a resource for acquiring new wisdom. Traditions are the residue of corporate experience of earlier Christian communities. A critical appreciation of them can enlarge our vision and enrich faith in God's provident love."
9. The test of experience is referred to in *The Book of Discipline, 1972*, p. 77, as follows: "There is a radical distinction between intellectual assent to the message of the Bible and doctrinal propositions set forth in creeds, and the personal experience of God's pardoning and healing love."
10. The test of reason is referred to in *The Book of Discipline, 1972*, page 78, as follows: "Christian doctrines which are developed from Scripture, tradition, and experience must be submitted to critical analysis so that they may commend themselves to thoughtful persons as valid."
11. *Ventures*, p. 48. From Deane Postlethwaite, the Good Samaritan United Methodist Church, Minneapolis.

4. Reality and Language

1. Willard L. Sperry observed this problem in his work *Reality in Worship* (New York: Macmillan, 1928.) See especially p. 222. While Sperry's book does not deal with the metaphysical aspect of the question as such, it remains illuminating on the practical side.

Peter Berger and Thomas Luckmann, *The Social Construction of Reality: A Treatise in the Sociology of Knowledge* (Garden City, N. Y.: Doubleday, 1966).

The question of reality is very much before the public today, thanks to people like Carlos Castaneda, whose experiments with Indian culture and drugs have convinced him that there is a "non-ordinary reality." See Castaneda, *The Teachings of Don Juan: A Yaqui Way of Knowledge* (New York: Ballantine Books, 1969), and *A Separate Reality* (Ballantine Books, 1972).

A fascinating study of how contemporary constructs of reality challenge tradition may be found in Joseph Chilton Pearce, *The Crack in the Cosmic Egg* (New York: Pocket Books, 1973).
2. See especially *Lectures on the Philosophy of History* by G. W. F.

141

Hegel, trans. J. Sibree (New York: Dover Publications, 1956).

3. See Søren Kierkegaard, *Concluding Unscientific Postcript to the Philosophical Fragments*, trans. David Swenson and Walter Lowrie (Princeton: Princeton University Press, 1944), especially p. 261.

4. James E. Edie, introduction to *What is Phenomenology?* by Pierre Thevanaz (Chicago: Quadrangle Books, 1962), p. 19. The basic work here is Edmund Husserl, *Ideas: General Introduction to Pure Phenomenology*, trans. W. R. Boyce Gibson (New York: Collier, 1962).

5. Karl Jaspers, *Way to Wisdom* (New Haven: Yale University Press, 1954), p. 74.

6. Micks, *The Future Present: The Phenomenon of Christian Worship* (New York: The Seabury Press, 1970) and Snyder, *Contemporary Celebration* (Nashville: Abingdon Press 1971).

7. Daniel B. Stevick has located a crisis in worship in language. See his study, *Language in Worship* (New York: The Seabury Press, 1970). Stevick deals with what we are distinguishing here as verbal language. His work is most helpful in clarifying verbal rather than nonverbal communication.

8. *Letters and Papers from Prison*, trans. Reginald Fuller and revised by Frank Clarke *et al.*, ed. Eberhard Bethge (New York: Macmillan, 1967), p. 172.

9. *Existence and Being*, with an introduction by Werner Brock (Chicago: Regnery, 1949), p. 276.

10. Fuchs, *Studies of the Historical Jesus*, trans. Andrew Scobbie (London: SCM Press, 1964), pp. 207-8.

11. Julius, Fast, *Body Language* (New York: M. Evans and Co., 1970). Bernard Gunther presents a most creative approach to more complete communication in his work *What to Do Till the Messiah Comes* (New York: Collier Books, 1971).

12. James F. White, *New Forms of Worship* (Nashville: Abingdon Press, 1971), especially "Environment of Worship," pp. 80-99. Compare White's *Protestant Worship and Church Architecture* (New York: Oxford University Press, 1964).

13. See Marge Champion and Marilee Zdenek, *Catch the New Wind: The Church Is Alive and Dancing* (Waco, Tex.: Word Books, 1972).

14. This film of the *Credo* is on 16 mm. sound film and is available from Dance Films, 250 West 57th St., N. Y. 10019, or The Project on Worship, P. O. Box 840, Nashville, Tenn. 37202.

15. All the above music may be found in *Ventures in Song*, ed. David J. Randolph with special assistance from Bill Garrett (Nashville: Abingdon Press, 1972).

16. (London: SCM Press, 1958.)

17. (Nashville: Abingdon Press, 1969.)

18. See David J. Randolph, *The Renewal of Preaching* (Philadelphia: Fortress Press, 1969), pp. 75-96.

19. *A Greek-English Lexicon of the New Testament and other Early Christian Literature*, trans. and adapted by William F. Arndt and F. Wilbur Gingrich (Chicago: The University of Chicago Press, 1957), pp. 19-25.

Notes

20. See *Understanding Media* (Signet; New York: New American Library, 1964). Compare McLuhan, *Hot and Cool*, Gerald E. Stearn, ed. (New York: Dial Press, 1967). For a discussion of how increased use of media might affect congregational worship, see Thor Hall, *The Future Shape of Preaching* (Philadelphia: Fortress Press, 1971).
21. See *Unfinished Man and the Imagination* (New York: The Seabury Press, 1968), p. 304.
22. *Visual Thinking* (Berkeley: University of California Press, 1969).
23. Sergei Eisenstein, *Film Form and Film Sense* (New York: Harcourt Brace and Co., 1942), p. 71.
24. See Wolfgang Kohler, *Gestalt Psychology* (New York: Livcright Publishing Corporation, 1929), or the discussion of Gestalt psychology by Edna Heidbreder in *Seven Psychologies* (New York and London: D. Appleton Century Co., 1933) See also Frederick Perls, Ralph F. Hefferline, and Paul Goodman, *Gestalt Therapy* (New York: Julian Press, 1951, 1971).

5 Values in the Verbal

1. For a study of proclamation as interpretation employing a multilayered structure see my work, *The Renewal of Preaching* (Philadelphia: Fortress Press, 1969). For a sampling of contemporary explorations of forms see John Killenger, ed., *Experimental Preaching* (Nashville: Abingdon Press, 1973).
2. See Arnheim, *Visual Thinking*, and Jurgen Ruesch and Weldon Kees *Non Verbal Communication* (Berkeley: University of California Press, 1972).
3. Caroline Spurgeon, *Shakespeare's Imagery: And What It Tells Us* (New York: Macmillan, 1935), p. 9
4. Wesley Taylor, Project on Worship, Salem, Oregon.
5. *Ventures 3*, p. 88.
6. Rudolph Flesch, *The Art of Readable Writing* (New York: Harper, 1949), especially chapter 9: "An Ear for Writing." Flesch is aware that these speech patterns violate some of the old taboos of style, and suggests that they be used with care for maximum effect. Certainly the worship leader in choosing his language must know that it is designed primarily for the ear. Compare H. Grady Davis, *Design for Preaching* (Philadelphia: Muhlenberg Press, 1958.) See especially chapter 15, "Writing for the Ear."
7. *Ventures 2*, p. 48.
8. *Ventures 3*, p. 31.
9. *Ventures 3*, p. 81.
10. *Ventures 2*, p. 81.
11. *Ventures 3*, p. 56.
12. *Ventures 3*, p. 95.
13. *In The Minister's Workshop* (Nashville and New York: Abingdon-Cokesbury Press, 1944), p. 184.
14. H. D. Lewis, ed., *Clarity Is Not Enough: Essays in Criticism of*

143

Linguistic Philosophy (London: George Allen & Unwin, 1963.)

15. *Seven Types of Ambiguity* (London: Chatto and Windus, 1930).
16. *Ventures*, p. 10; from the First University United Methodist Church, Minneapolis.
17. *Ventures 3*, pp. 55-56.
18. J. L. Hevesi, ed. *Essays on Language and Literature* (London: Allan Wingate, 1947), pp. 152-53.
19. From Stephen Fink, Kansas Wesleyan University, Project on Worship.
20. *Ventures*, p. 18; from the First University United Methodist Church, Minneapolis.
21. See *Aesthetics and History* by Bernard Berenson (Garden City, N.Y.: Doubleday, 1954), p. 150.
22. *A Bed by the Sea* (Garden City, N. Y.: Doubleday, 1970), p. 87.
23. This story is drawn from the film *Gigot*, which was directed by its star, Jackie Gleason.

6. Worship in Joy and Sorrow

1. From Pastor Ken Gelhaus, Stoughton, Wisc., with David and Natalie Joranson. From the Project on Worship.
2. *Ventures 3*, pp. 163-65.
3. This discussion of baptism is drawn from my work entitled *Baptism: Historical, Theological and Practical Considerations* (Nashville: Abingdon Press, 1968).
4. David G. Owen, *Transparent Worship* (New York: Women's Division, Board of Global Ministries of The United Methodist Church n.d.), p. 84.
5. *An Order for the Celebration of Holy Baptism*, prepared by the Commission on Worship of the Consulation on Church Union (Cincinnati: Forward Publications, 1973).
6. *Ibid.*, pp. 173-74.
7. *The Worship Manual*, published by the Worship Commission of the Minnesota Annual Conference of The United Methodist Church, 122 West Franklin Avenue, Minneapolis, pp. 25-26.

7. How Do We Get to the Party?

1. See Joyce Carol Oates, "The Unique Universal and Fiction," *The Writer*, January, 1973, pp. 9-12. See also *The Creative Process*, a symposium edited by Brewster Chiselin (New York: Mentor Books, 1957-58), especially pp. 15-28; and Arthur Koestler, *The Act of Creation* (New York: Dell, 1967). Those interested in the process of creativity should look into George M. Prince, *The Practice of Creativity: A Manual for Dynamic Group Problem-Solving* (New York: Collier Books, 1972).
2. In correspondence with the author.
3. For an excellent case study of how one congregation transformed its worship see Dan Kennedy, "Worship—From Package to Probe," *Ventures 2*, pp. 191-220.
4. Quoted in Resource (United Church of Canada), June, 1971, p. 14.